Memories

of

Worcester

The publishers would like to thank the following companies for their
support in the production of this book

Armstrong of Worcester

Ebenezer Baylis & Son Limited

Bullock Buildbase

Robin Elt Shoes

A Forrest-Hay Limited

Froude Consine

The Alice Ottley School

GR Pratley & Son

B Smith Packaging (Worcester) Limited

Spicers (Builders) Limited

Taylors of Martley plc

First published in Great Britain by True North Books Limited
England HX5 9AE
Telephone: 01422 377977

ISBN 1 903204 25 9

Text, design and origination by True North Books Limited
Printed and bound in Great Britain

Memories

of

Worcester

Contents

Page 8

Street scenes

•

Page 33

On the move

•

Page 39

Events & occasions

•

Page 48

At leisure

•

Page 58

Shopping spree

•

Page 69

Making a living

Introduction

Sauce and quality china have made the name 'Worcester' a household name around the globe. But Worcester has far more than its traditional products to commend it, as those who live in the city know well, and this new collection of nostalgic images calls to mind the way we once lived in the Worcester of our youth.

We revisit the vanished places of entertainment such as the Scala - the scene, perhaps, of our first date? - and the historic Public Hall, which long ago hosted celebrities such as Charles Dickens, Jenny Lind, and Worcester's very own Sir Edward Elgar. We take a peep at some of the city's notable occasions such as the granting of the Freedom of the City to 'Good old Winnie' in 1950, and the visit of Princess Elizabeth in 1951, a mere seven months before she ascended the throne.

We take a trip down Memory Lane and take a look at the good times, from the charabanc trips made by our parents and grandparents to the pleasure steamers of old, which turned South Quay into a hive of activity (a leisure activity which has now come full circle!). We go on a shopping spree around stores which were destined to fall victim to road widening schemes or vanish below modern shopping complexes; we experience again the thrills and sawdust of Bertram Mills Circus, and wonder once more at the ingeniously decorated floats at the Worcester Carnival back in the 1960s.

There were, of course, the not so good times, when the people of Worcester squared their shoulders and simply got on with life. There were those long ago days of air raid shelters, make do and mend, ration books, and bananaless greengrocery stores. And the long-ago rain storms which turned our main roads into waterways and brought the city to a virtual standstill. And there was the roaring inferno - both seen and heard all around the city - which reduced the premises of the ironmongers J C Baker to blackened timbers, ash and rubble.

cont. overleaf

From previous page

Worcester has a rich history and tradition that goes back to the Roman era, the days when King John ordered the building of Edgar Tower and also encompasses the Civil War days of the 1600s, when our forbears fought at the Battle of Worcester and gave shelter to the troubled 'Black Boy', King Charles II. The city still has an abundance of historical sites and connections, though as a tourist centre of growing importance Worcester's future lies in preserving what we still have of the past. After all, we have already lost so much of it on the whim of those 1960s committees wielding red pens and suffering from delusions of competence.(Who was it who once said that a camel is a horse designed by a committee?)

We are well aware that we cannot progress without change, but is the city really better off without the old Public Hall, the beautiful half-timbered premises of J & F Hall in the Shambles, the Lich Gate, the nearby half-timbered buildings around Lich Street, and so many more of our old pubs, churches, and historic buildings? And has Worcester truly benefited from the addition of such architectural 'gems' as the Technical College and the angular tower blocks bequeathed to us by the clean sweep of the 1960s, which sit uncomfortably in our historic city like Santa Claus in July? Thankfully, our heritage has many survivors - as long ago as the 1940s the spire of St Andrew's narrowly escaped demolition when the bulldozers moved in on the church! It is vital that we remember that once a piece of history is razed to the ground there is no way of putting it back again....

Henry Ford was fond of telling his friends, 'Plan for the future, because that's where you're going to spend the rest of your life', and the committees of more recent times appear to have acquired the perfect vision of 20/20 hindsight. We can only applaud the more sympathetic planning which has recently endeavoured to compensate

for the mistakes of the past. Urban renewal has given us the Reindeer Court shopping centre, with its tasteful shops and cafes, the Crowngate shopping complex with its large chain stores and market, and the beautifully converted Hop Market, where tourists and residents alike can browse in the smart gift shops around the old courtyard. Regeneration certainly has its compensations, and recent years have seen the canalside and riverside alike transformed from an unpleasant mix of scrap yards, mud and scrub to delightful circular walks, pleasant river cruises, and summer visitors enjoying 'messing about in boats'.

Worcester has much to attract the visitor: its beautiful cathedral, founded by St Oswald as a Saxon monastery in the year 983, and the burial place of King John; the 13th Century Edgar Tower with its original massive wooden gateway still in place; the Commandery, used by Charles II as his headquarters during the Battle of Worcester in 1651; the handsome Guildhall, which was designed by Thomas White, a student of Sir Christopher Wren, in

1721, and the Royal Worcester factory and the Dyson Perrins Museum of rare porcelain. Lovers of the arts have the Swan Theatre and the Huntingdon, where they can experience the best in music, dance and drama, and sporting enthusiasts have a choice of the National Hunt meetings at Worcester Racecourse, first class cricket played in the shadow of the Cathedral, St George's Lane for football or a visit to Sixways to watch the Gold 'n Blues play Premiership League rugby.

We are fortunate indeed that the 20th Century was so well chronicled, and we have only to compare our present city, with its exciting developments in sport and leisure, commerce and the arts, with Worcester as it was, say in the 1940s, to see what progress has been realised and what achievements have been made over the last 60 or so years. Worcester has a history we can all be proud of - and just as importantly, a great future to look forward to. We hope that you will read and enjoy 'Memories of Worcester' - and remember that history is still in the making.

Street scenes

No fluorescent jacket for this traffic bobby; a pair of white gloves and sleeves was sufficient to gain the attention of the 1920s driver. Back then, every major junction in every major town had its police officer on point duty; remember those black and white zebra-striped boxes they often used? But one by one they disappeared, leaving us with a trail of traffic lights at every major road junction. Efficient the computerised lights may be, but somehow they lack the personal touch of the good old traffic bobby.

This one is on duty on the corner of Broad Street and The Cross, and Hepworths' outfitters behind him were having their annual sale. Their offer of 4/- and £1 off overcoats would have been well worth looking at. Gentlemen's outfitting has long been a trade to attract many rivals; Masters & Co were in the same trade (though not so upmarket) just two doors away. Hepworths eventually managed to acquire the services of the Queen's own designer. This shop is today a branch of H Samuel - further along The Cross at the time of our photograph - while the adjoining Lipton's grocery store vanished from the scene a long time ago. Their signs are worth a mention; today they would not be able to claim that 'Lipton's butter is the best'!

Above: A suit for 37 shillings - the size of the sign in Burton's window indicates that this was a good price even in the 1920s. Montague Burton's good quality menswear has been a traditional favourite with gentlemen for many years, and virtually every town and city in Britain has at least one branch. The story goes that when soldiers were demobbed after military service they were given vouchers to be outfitted at Burtons. They went along to the nearest branch and were kitted out in what was termed 'the full Monty' - a phrase which has in recent years come to mean something very different from a full suit of clothes!

Few readers will remember The Cross at the time of the photograph; the short flight of steps which once graced the entrance to St Nicholas' Church can be seen on the left. There are more pedestrians in the view than vehicles, and this was a fair reflection of the 1920s, when a private car was an undreamed of luxury and virtually everyone travelled by tram. Our view is unfortunately undated, but the tram lines suggest that this was some time before 1928, when the Midland Red bus company took over as Worcester's public transport.

Right: The rattle of teacups has today replaced the rustle of hymn books, but although God is no longer worshipped in St Nicholas' church at least the building itself has been preserved. Dominating our 1951 photograph of The Cross, the magnificent tower of St Nicholas' Church is a fine sight, and a landmark of which Worcester can be proud. The church and its splendid tower which we know today were constructed during the 1730s, built to replace a 12th century church which once stood on the same site. In medieval times The Cross was very much the centre of Worcester. Here in the hub of the town's activities stood an engraved cross - and here, too, were Worcester's stocks, where petty crime was punished. Fun for the townspeople who turned up to throw rotten eggs and the odd dead cat, but a bit grim for the person on the receiving end! Eight hundred years later The Cross was a very different place, and by 1951 the motor car was on its way to ruling supreme. Car design had a long way to go, however, and the mid 1950s would see many changes introduced as the mudguards and running boards seen here became a thing of the past.

This pleasant view south-east across Worcester dates from 1960, and many familiar features such as the elegant spire of St Andrew's, the former Hounds Lane School in Deansway, and Worcester Cathedral, can still be picked out. The intervening years have of course seen the building of the Technical College on the left bank of the river. Few readers will fail to recognise the little tableau on the right as being echoed on Britain's £20 notes - increasing the value, no doubt, of the house in front of the Cathedral! The bridge over the Severn has been part of Worcester's history since 1781 - and its building

was not as straightforward as had been originally hoped. Work on the bridge, designed by the prominent 18th century designer John Gwynn in his later years, met with one complication after another: the arches had to be redesigned as they would have been too low to cope with flooding; slow contractors failed to stick to deadlines; prices escalated - and the bridge took 10 years to complete. The finished work, however, was an ornament to the city - though Gwynne had to shame the trustees into paying his agreed commission, and an outstanding debt of £600 was still owed to him when he died in 1786.

The Cross had a host of shops and services to offer Worcester: you could purchase an engagement ring, have your wedding suit made, fill your camera with Kodak film, purchase after-dinner cigars for the celebration, buy your breakfast bacon for the morning after, and take afternoon tea at the Vigornia Cafe, all within the space of a hundred yards or so.

How many of those 'lucky' wedding rings purchased from H Samuel in 1928 still survive? And did they bring their owners the promised good luck? A gift was given with each wedding ring purchased; half a dozen silver teaspoons, perhaps, or a pair of napkin rings. In those days H Samuel went in for advertising in a way they probably would not today!

This remarkable photograph was taken on 9th April 1928, and scores of people line the kerbsides, presumably waiting for buses, while a traffic jam has developed as motorists head out towards Stratford, Malvern and Hereford. That busy Easter there would have been a big demand for the Midland Red Motor Tours, with crowds of eager day trippers taking advantage of a rare day's holiday from the office or the shop.

Left: Remember The Shades Inn in Mealcheapen Street? And the Reindeer as it used to be? No hint in our nostalgic photograph of the enormous changes which were to bring Reindeer Court Shopping Centre to the city! The Reindeer was a very ancient coaching inn which dates back at least to the 17th Century - and possibly even earlier than that, and in its early years it was known as The Rayned Deer. The Shades, which stood virtually opposite, began life, as so many inns did, as a private house. In its long history it has been the home of the prominent 18th Century Russell family, a coffee house, The Shades Tavern, and Worcester's first post office before reverting, in the 20th century, to its earlier use as an inn. It was here that Edward Elgar's father and mother are reputed to have met. Mealcheapen Street was particularly quiet when the photographer recorded this view, for which we unfortunately have no date. Three lone pedestrians were all that stirred, in spite of the shops appearing to be open; Scholl's on the right has its sun blind down to protect the goods in the window. Early in the morning, or closing time in the evening? We can only speculate.

Above: One horsepower traffic in The Cross - not a sight we see today! But this was 1951, and although the internal combustion engine had already left the old methods of transport far behind, the odd horse and cart could still be seen. The sight puts us in mind of those gentler days when noise from the city's vehicles involved only the rattle of wheels and the clopping of hooves, and the only traffic pollution could be put to good use on your floribundas! With St Nicholas' Church and the Cadena Cafe - always a popular meeting place - to the right, the view looks north towards the railway bridge. A fashionable young lady on the left of the photograph is keeping up with the fashions of the day, which by 1950 had begun to change as widely flared skirts replaced the shorter styles of the austere war years. Mid calf length skirts were the 'in thing', together with the short, soft perm and Louis heels. Remember paper nylon underskirts? And those frothy net ones? Lady readers who were in their teens and twenties during the 1950s certainly will. And perhaps our male readers will remember with nostalgia those occasional tantalising glimpses of foaming petticoat!

Bottom: Blessedly free of traffic - this was a Foregate Street that only the more mature readers will be familiar with, caught on camera around 1925. The fascinating glimpse through time reminds us that slender ankles were only just being revealed by the ladies' skirts, and that virtually no-one went out of doors without a hat! The old electric open top trams which might still be remembered by a few stopped running in May 1928. Imagine how wet and uncomfortable they would have been on rainy days! The tram drivers were even worse off than the passengers, as trams had no windscreens until the late 1930s. It was quickly recognised that trams - and later buses - made ideal mobile advertisement hoardings, and soap, tea, mustard and local stores were just a few of the products brought to the attention of the potential customer. The tram in our photograph advertises Bovril, and the early Bovril slogans were not without a touch of humour ('I hear they want more!' says one nervous bull to another). Their ingenuity made Bovril into a household name. Interestingly, the catchphrase 'Bovril prevents that sinking feeling' was designed before World War I but was withheld at the time as a mark of respect for the families of those lost on the 'Titanic' in 1912.

Right: With her back to the Shire Hall, Queen Victoria, regally carrying the symbolic orb and sceptre, gazes impassively across the car park towards the passing Foregate Street traffic. The statue, carved from a 17 ton block of marble, was set here to commemorate the Queen's Golden Jubilee in 1890.

Victoria was just 18 years old when she came to the throne, and she reigned for 64 years, which was longer than any other British monarch. The Shire Hall was opened in 1838 as the Worcestershire County Council headquarters, and the imposing classical-style building with its magnificent Corinthian columns cost a total of £32,000. A snip, we might think, with today's property prices in mind - but a pound would buy you many more bricks and mortar back in the mid 19th century! The fine old vehicles in our photograph parked carefully within the painted lines outside the Shire Hall point to the 1930s; the cars might have been superb, but what a lot of petrol these monsters must have used! The iron railings seen here survived the World War II campaign for scrap iron, but have recently been sympathetically replaced with similar ones.

Above: The Old Pheasant in New Street has a history that dates back as far as the 17th Century, and its ancient walls have no doubt been witness to many a fascinating scene. Was the old tavern once the haunt of secret Royalists, who in the days of bleak Puritanism daringly drunk to the health of Charles II? After the execution of his father Charles I, the King in waiting lived his life travelling around Europe, hoping that one day he would be able to return to England as King. His one attempt to gain the throne by force in 1651 met with failure, and not far away in New Street is King Charles House, from where Charles II escaped Cromwell's troops in the nick of time after the Battle of Worcester.

A little detective work tells us that the original owner of the Old Pheasant was probably a wealthy citizen of the city: the building's timbers have been placed closer together than necessary - a feature known as 'close studding' - and reveal the fact that 'oneupmanship' is not restricted to the 21st Century!

The Old Pheasant is only one of the area's ancient buildings. A mere stone throw away lies the Swan with Two Nicks, another old inn which was listed as being in the city back in 1793.

Below centre: Remember the time when you could leave your bike at the kerbside or leaning against a wall, and expect it to be still there when you returned? Those were the days! The owners of these particular cycles were probably browsing among the works of Conan Doyle or P G Wodehouse, confident in the assumption that they would be able to ride home again after their visit to the library. Whether you wanted to unwind with Ernest Hemingway or enjoyed the edge-of-the-seat excitement of Agatha Christie, there was something in the library to suit your taste in fiction, while an extensive selection of non-fiction would give you information about wide-ranging topics.

The Victoria Institute - surely one of Worcester's most beautiful buildings - was built to honour Queen Victoria's Golden Jubilee, which she celebrated in 1887. The Duke of York, later to become King George V, visited Worcester in 1894 to lay the foundation stone. The Institute, would one day house not only the library but the city's museum and art gallery, adding an exciting development to Worcester's rich culture, was just two years in the building, and it was opened in October 1896 by the Mayoress, Lady Mary Lygon.

Doesn't it seem strange to see traffic in High Street? This busy shopping scene was caught on camera in August 1968. The passing cars are typical of the day, and the fact that two of them are Triumph Heralds reminds us of just how popular they were. How many readers remember owning one in their younger days? Between them is a little Austin A35, which cost around £900 new. Marks and Spencer and Woolworths appears to be as busy as usual; you will perhaps remember the devastating fire that later destroyed this Woolworths building. Marks & Spencer has suffered from an unfortunate 'fuddy-duddy' image in recent years, but the quality of its clothing has never been in doubt, and M & S remains the favourite store with thousands of shoppers. Marks and Spencer began life in Britain in the early years of the 20th century when Marks' Penny Bazaar opened up in the market in Leeds, West Yorkshire. Founders Michael Marks & Tom Spencer opened their first shops under the name of Penny Bazaar, and by 1915 Messrs Marks & Spencer had set up 140 Penny Bazaars throughout the country - not a bad rate of return from an investment of £300!

Photograph by Michael Dowty

Photograph by Michael Dowty

Left: St Swithin's Street was busy with its usual mix of shoppers, motorists and delivery vehicles (spot the wagon loaded with milk churns in the background) when this view was captured at the beginning of August 1968 - and it was rather cool for an English summer day, judging by the coats worn by the cheerfully smiling girls in the shot. To quote an over-used cliche, what goes around comes around, and the short, above-the-knee length skirts sported by these young ladies have once more gained popularity - and are today being worn, no doubt, by their daughters! The view takes us back to the shops of our younger days; how many of our readers remember shopping at the International Stores? And choosing paint and wallpaper at Decorwall on the right? It was during the 1960s that DIY began to take a firm foothold with young couples who wanted to create their 'dream home', and Decorwall, to the right, would have been one of their first ports of call. The fine building facing the camera in the centre of the photograph has since been listed, and participates in the city's recent policy of encouraging families to live above city centre shops.

Below: Babyland was already on its way out when this scene was recorded around 1963 - and was sadly missed by young mums shopping for supplies for their new little ones. For those younger readers who may have difficulty placing the location, this was Friar Street, taken from Lich Street. Looking towards Sidbury, Hunt's Leather Stores - a well known Worcester firm - was on the left, as was Multi Broadcast TV rentals and Johnson's Sound Service. Further along we can just spot the sign outside the Esso station. Almost opposite stands the old Talbot, one of the country's most ancient inns. The Talbot was playing host to visitors to Worcester when William Shakespeare first set pen to paper, and the old tavern is still with us today, though in a vastly altered form. The Talbot was an establishment simply begging to have the prefix 'Ye Olde' tacked on to it, and so it was, somewhere along the line. Back in the 1960s bed and breakfast at the old inn would have set you back 35/- (£1.75), while a pleasant evening dinner could be had for 12/6d (around 62 ½p). Sounds a bargain, doesn't it - until you take the average take-home pay of the day into consideration!

Many of the buildings in this shot, which dates from February 1965, are still with us today, though the road layout has been changed and the Lychgate Precinct built. Well worth mentioning is the house with the high pediment facing us, once the girlhood home of the famous Victorian novelist Mrs Henry Wood, the daughter of Thomas Price, a glove manufacturer. It may be that some younger readers are not familiar with Mrs Wood and her writings, but her most famous (or infamous?) book, 'East Lynne' was rejected by two publishers before it saw the light of

day in 1861. The story of the beautiful young wife seduced by a handsome but contemptible cad was regarded as scandalous in the strictly moralistic climate of the day - resulting, of course, in it becoming a best seller. The full-blooded story of passion and intrigue (and which was based on a true event) is a ripping yarn which is even today well worth a read. A certain fiction about 'East Lynne' has grown up over the years - Lady Isabel, on the death of her son, never did utter the much quoted misquote that tradition has assigned to her: 'Dead! - and never called me Mother!'

Below: A sight to stir many memories of school speech days, carol concerts and election addresses - the Majestic, once the Public Hall. It fell victim to the red pen of the city planners in the mid 1960s, and by 1966 the building which had once been the ill-fated corn exchange was a heap of rubble. It was sad to see so much of the city's history disappear. After all, so much of it was made within these walls! Here the famous Charles Dickens himself performed readings from 'The Pickwick Papers' and 'A Christmas Carol' back in 1867; Elgar conducted 'The Enigma Variations' and Dvorak his Stabat Mater, and here the Swedish operatic soprano Johanna Maria Lind - known to us all as 'Jenny Lind, the Swedish Nightingale' - wowed the audience in a fund raising concert for the Worcester Royal Infirmary. A public car park was the Hall's ignominious end, but there has been campaigning recently among those who would like to see the area turned into a public square once more, as it was in the days of the old corn market. For many years the corn market was a hive of activity - and not just for trade. This was a place of fairs, fun - and public floggings!

Right: When the timber framed building occupied by ironmongers J & F Hall Ltd was demolished, many were the voices raised in protest against this act of 'Whitehall vandalism'. J & F Hall had occupied this same building since the late 19th Century and are well remembered in the city. Local DIY enthusiasts still think wistfully of Halls - the place where they could browse undisturbed and stock up on all their needs, whether they had popped in to choose their door furniture, buy a set of shelf brackets, pick up a couple of dozen galvanised nails or acquire a set of cup hooks. The unusual carving underneath the clock atop St Swithun's church echoes the 14th Century 'green man' in the Cathedral cloisters - and also that on the inn sign outside the 'Green Man' in The Tything. Isn't it amazing how familiarity can breed, if not contempt, at least inattention? Far below the clock - which informs us that the time is 10.55am - preoccupied shoppers in The Shambles are going about their business, so used to seeing St Swithun's church that they rarely if ever stop to admire the handsome frontage of the church with its fine Venetian window.

The names above the shop windows may have changed, and the traffic has probably more than doubled, but the buildings remain in essence virtually the same. This view of the west side of The Tything was recorded on 12th April 1965. The tiny 'Green Man' pub continues to cater for the thirst of the local citizens of Worcester, as does the Lamb & Flag, about 100 yds further along, and both the old inns are very much part of the history of the city. The Green Man

Photograph by Michael Dowty

was listed as being in Worcester back in 1793, and interestingly the inn had a still until the middle of the 19th Century, where herbalists used to distill their brews. Did they also sell them from there, we wonder? The sign of the Green Man is so similar to the 14th Century carving in the Cathedral that it has to have been modelled on it, though the reason for reproducing the image is not known to us. The Lamb & Flag has been with us since the 19th Century, when it was known as the Old Lamb & Fleece.

A tree near the Cathedral acts as an advertising hoarding, informing passers-by of a pre-Christmas treat - the 'Messiah' was to be performed on 14th December 1962. We can assume that this particular production was to take place at the Cathedral itself, though literally hundreds of churches, village choirs and operatic societies up and down the country would have been busy practising for their own performance of Handel's famous oratorio. Handel, German-born but a naturalised Briton, was one of those rare artists who was famous in his own time, and people looked forward to his latest piece of music with the same enthusiasm that meets today's new popular songs. The Messiah was written, so the story goes, because Handel needed the money - but it quickly established itself as a firm favourite. And who, even today, is not familiar with the marvellous 'Hallelujah Chorus'? Our pre-1966 shot of College Street captures the view before the Lychgate development changed the scene for ever, with the Old Talbot Inn serving Flowers' ales in the background.

Right: Still 'fanatical about film', the Odeon cinema continues to provide the picture-goers of Worcester with first class entertainment. Down the years, the Odeon in Foregate Street has been a

Photograph by Michael Dowty

photograph. Today, Baker's building has been rebuilt in smart red brick and is occupied by a pizza takeaway, while a pelican crossing has replaced the nearby zebra crossing.

survivor. It escaped the devastating fire that swept through the nearby premises of ironmongers J C Baker in June 1966 - still supported by scaffolding in our photograph. It also survived the 'cinema slump' which was brought on by the widespread popularity of television during the 1950s. Those were bad years for the cinema, and hundreds of establishment made an attempt to survive by going eyes down to bingo. Few made it through to the late 1990s, by which time the tide was turning once more in favour of cinema-going. Today's trend has largely been towards the out of town multi-screen cinemas which are mushrooming around many of our cities, where additional on-site facilities offer such attractions as drive-in burger bars and under-cover shopping centres. Thankfully, the Odeon was able to keep going. 'The Devil Rides Out', starring Christopher Lee, was being screened at the time of this

Below: An unusual photograph, this one, as double deck buses did not survive for long in Worcester. We are informed that this view was captured at 8.45am on 3rd August 1968, and considering the fact that the day is still young the driver of this Number W1 bound for Ombersley Road looks remarkably fed up. Perhaps the same feeling afflicted the owners of these barrows and ladders; have they deserted their buckets, their chamois leathers and their ladders, we wonder, and gone off somewhere to snatch a quick mug of tea and a bacon butty? After all, dirty windows can wait! Readers will perhaps remember the old International Stores, sadly long gone along with other grocery chains, to be replaced by out of town supermarkets. At least the Hop Market Hotel survived along with the hop market itself, and in an ambitious modernisation scheme became a rather stylish fashion shop.

Photograph by Michael Dowty

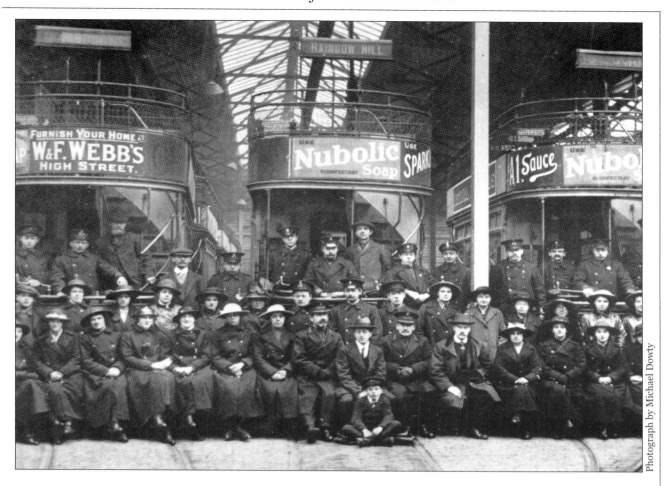

Photograph by Michael Dowty

On the move

Worcester electric tramways was an 'almost equal opportunities' employer, as we can see from this undated photograph of over 20 female and over 20 male staff. Was the little chap sitting in front the company's mascot, we wonder? The young ladies, each with their ankles demurely crossed and wearing an elegant hat, formed an important part of the workforce though it's doubtful that any of them ever drove a tram. These, no doubt, were the conductresses (and perhaps some office girls), proud of having a job which took them away from the drudgery of the kitchen sink and gave them a certain amount of independence - though their wages would have been well below that of the male staff! The changeover from the old horse trams to an electrified system was not made without a good deal of inconvenience, as the old rails, laid to a 3ft gauge, had to be dug up and replaced with the new 3ft 6ins gauge (which interestingly differed from the standard British gauge of 4ft 8½ins), and the city was in chaos for months. But early in 1904 the first routes were ready for use and the new service was opened on 6th February, with a standard fare of 1d. The Midland Red Omnibus Company took over from the trams on 1st June 1928.

Left: South Quay was a hive of activity when this marvellous scene was captured, though unfortunately for us the photograph bears no date. Busy at the masthead of this smart little vessel, a man fixes festoons of fairy lights; whatever the special occasion (and the shirt sleeves and bare arms indicate that it was not Christmas), the overall effect would have been stunning after dark.

A couple of hundred years ago the Severn was a commercial highway, alive with vessels transporting goods - a situation which changed dramatically with the laying down of railway lines. After the advent of the railway, traffic on the river became mainly pleasure craft as people discovered the delights of cruising, and crowded pleasure steamers were a common sight on the Severn. But this, too, had its day, and as families began to acquire cars and travel further the number of steamers on the river diminished. Recent years, however, have seen people turning once more to the water, and river cruises from the North Quay number among the activities Worcester has on offer.

Below: Worcester, along with the rest of the country, was in the grip of flower power when this view was captured on 3rd August 1968. The 'sixties were swinging for the trendy young couple on the scooter, though older people were no doubt scandalised by the length of the girl's skirt! Motor cycle helmets were not thought to be important 30-odd years ago, and although her gauzy white scarf might have kept the girl's hair in place it would have been as much use as a chocolate fireguard in an accident! The Hop Market Hotel has been a familiar sight on the corner of Foregate and St Nicholas Street for many years. The present fine terracotta building dates from 1900, when together with the new hopmarket it was built to replace an 18th Century hotel which was demolished in a road-widening scheme. Many readers will still remember watching the pockets of hops being hoisted up on the gantry in the nearby hop market - and that occasional thrill of horror when one of them swung inwards, breaking a window! Today the Hop Market Hotel is a rather smart clothes shop, while the hop market itself has been turned into a series of small shops and a cafe built around the old courtyard.

Photograph by Michael Dowty

This page: Croft Road was awash when a photographer - wearing wellington boots we hope - set up his camera and snapped this little drama taking place below the arches of the viaduct *(bottom)*. (The first railway arch to be built on the skew can be seen on the left of the view.) The resulting photograph, dated around 1964, reveals that motorists are driving as much towards the centre of the road as they can, and pedestrians and cyclists are keeping to the pavements, where things are slightly drier. But the little knots of people on both sides of the road have quite literally come up against a problem: how to get past the supporting columns of the viaduct without having to step into the floodwater. Without the aid of a pair of wings or a sympathetic driver, however, they are undoubtedly going to get their feet wet!

What were conditions like on the racecourse, just beyond the trees in our picture? Built on the banks of the River Severn, the ground could well have been more than a little soft that day - though we trust that there were no fish swimming around on the track. If so, it wouldn't have been the first time that fish have been found in strange places after one of Worcester's famous floods; the great flood of 1947 left piles of lamperns (a kind of river lamprey) behind at the power station in Hylton Road, which dominates the background of our second view *(right)*. Not slow to recognise an opportunity, the staff duly gathered up the fish (20 buckets of them) and sold them for a ha'penny each. Many a family

would have had fried lamperns for tea that day, but we have no information about what these more unusual fish with leech-like mouths tasted like, or whether they were worth the ha'penny charged. We still see spectacular flooding from time to time (as in the Autumn of 2000), but the 1947 flood, as recorded on the wall beside the Watergate, was the highest in the city's history. The flooding turned Hylton Road into a waterway, and the only way to negotiate it without getting wet was by boat! Then of course when the flood water eventually subsided the mopping up operations began. People's homes and businesses were a sea of smelly mud that was messy to deal with and difficult to get rid of. Roads awash with water have long been an unfortunate but familiar sight in and around Worcester, and long rainy spells are still dreaded by those luckless people whose homes are situated in low lying areas.

Above: Let's be honest now; we have to admit that with a little more thought and attention to the kerbside this car could have been better parked. And with a little more thought and attention to road signs the driver might have spotted the fact that Exchange Street was a one-way street - the other way! The driver of BPK 958B is obviously not expecting any interference from traffic wardens or passing police officers! Never mind, perhaps he has merely jumped out to ask a passing pedestrian the way - after all, he could well be a 'foreigner', a theory supported by the fact that his number plate bears a Surrey registration. That would explain a lot.... At least he has had the grace not to park on the double yellow lines! Yellow no-waiting lines came into force for the first time on 16th June 1958. It doesn't seem so long ago, does it? It was fortunate that apart from a bus in the distance Exchange Street was traffic free at the time of the photograph, which dates from 1970. Since then we have lost the buildings in the right foreground, one of which formed part of the premises of J & F Hall Ltd, the well known ironmongers.

Below: Why use an official car park when you can park outside it for free? Of course, the official one might not be a 'pay and display' facility (there was a time when free car parks did exist!), but even so, half a dozen cars have rejected it in favour of the empty space adjoining it. As cities grow, and buildings are constructed, fewer and fewer such open spaces remain to the frustrated motorist who often wonders why, in an expanding universe, he can never find a parking space! This vista would eventually be changed by the building of Kay & Co's huge new office block. Established in Worcester around 1800, Kay's mail order company became a major employer in the area. Kay's has been one of the city's success stories as households across the country have chosen their new clothes and shoes, furniture and electrical goods from the famous glossy catalogue. Shrub Hill Railway Station can be seen in the background. Tastefully built to blend with its surroundings, the station's elegant facade more closely resembles a row of Georgian style houses.

This undated photograph raises more questions than it answers. The large number of marvellous old vehicles leads us to the obvious conclusion that a special event was taking place, but we are left in doubt as to exactly what the occasion was. The cricket ground appears to be empty, so we can discount the theory of an important match taking place. Could the scene perhaps have been recorded on 28 October 1932, the day the Prince of Wales came to open the newly-widened City Bridge? Henry Ford promised 'any colour car as long as it is black', and black was certainly the predominant colour among these wonderful old motors, with only the white BFH 597 to thwart a 100 per cent tally! It was during the 1950s that car design became really innovative. A variety of colours appeared, and mudguards and running boards like the ones on these old 'sit up and beg' motors were set to become a thing of the past.

Thankfully, this idyllic pastoral scene remains unspoilt today: open meadows and the cricket ground, presided over by Worcester's majestic Cathedral. But recent talk of the building of a new Cricket School leaves us to wonder how long this will remain to us....

Events & occasions

'**G**R' are the initials picked out in lights on Worcester Bridge to welcome King George VI to the throne. The coronation celebrations held on 12th May 1937, however, were not those originally planned. In the event the monarch being crowned was not Edward VIII, who Britain had expected to reign after the death of King George V, but his younger brother, Albert, Duke of York. Prince Albert, a shy and retiring family man who suffered from an embarrassing stammer, had been catapulted on to the throne when Edward abdicated to marry the twice-divorced Wallis Simpson. Edward had been a charming and popular man - but Worcester was determined to be loyal to the new sovereign. So the name was changed, the illuminations, the banners and the bunting all went up, and the street parties went ahead as originally planned. Though the new King had never seen a state paper in his life, he rose to the challenge, squared his shoulders, and went on to take his place as one of Britain's most well loved monarchs.

Beautifully reflecting the soft light against the blackness of the night sky, the spire of St Andrew's, the 'Glover's Needle', points upwards to the night sky. The church was still a place of worship at the time of the photograph, and the famous spire narrowly escaped demolition when the church was pulled down in the 1940s.

Above: Few of us realise that Charles II was only 21 years old when he attempted to gain the throne in 1651, though any Worcester school child knows about his humiliating defeat at the Battle of Worcester, and how he took refuge in the house that now bears his name. As his enemies entered by the front door, he escaped at the back - or so the story goes. The plaque commemorating the King's escape was unveiled by the Mayor with due ceremony in 1953, and was duly recorded on film for posterity. Note the oak branch mounted above the door, and the symbolic 'buttonholes' of oak leaves worn by the officials in the photograph. Readers will no doubt be already familiar with the story of the hollow oak in the grounds of Boscobel House in Salop, which for six long weeks provided another refuge for the beleaguered young king, who eventually fled to France. The oak which survives there today was grown from an acorn from the original tree.

Part of the King Charles House - built in 1577 - was destroyed by fire in the 18th Century. It was later restored and turned into a restaurant, and today visitors can enjoy a pleasant meal in the building that once played host to the Merry Monarch.

Right: Were you in Worcester on the day J C Bakers' burnt down? If so you will not have forgotten the billowing black smoke and the thunderous boom and crash of the exploding calor gas cylinders and drums of paint, which could be heard all around the city. It was 2nd June 1966 when a small fire inside the shop quickly spread into a mighty inferno. As the immense pall of smoke rose above Foregate Street, the fire brigade leaped into action and were quickly on the scene, their engines racing to both the back and front of the store. Evacuation was a priority, and the public were asked to leave the buildings nearby, including the Odeon cinema. Rather more difficult was the removal of a large number of animals from the vet's! Baker's huge stock of Calor gas and paint - not to mention the hundreds of gallons of paraffin stored inside what was one of the city's major ironmongers - made this an exceptionally ugly fire to fight, and the blaze was at its height, with hoses snaking across Farrier Street at the rear of the building, when this scene was captured on camera. The building was eventually rebuilt, and today is one of the area's many fast food takeaways.

Fifty years on, and these veterans of the Battle of Gheluvelt and their wives gather in front of the Guildhall to watch the commemorative parade march by. 'The gallant Worcesters' were justifiably proud of their achievements: the first world war may well have been lost as early as October 1914 had the Worcester Regiment not prevented the Germans from breaking through the British Expeditionary Force in an action once described as 'perhaps the finest exploit of any single battalion in the whole of World War I'. There were many acts of selflessness and heroism, but the battle was not fought without its losses, and the proud ex-servicemen pictured here had their bitter memories to look back on as well as their good ones. After the parade they moved on to the Cathedral, where a special service of thanksgiving was held - and there was much for them to give thanks for. Where many towns and cities simply erected war memorials to remember those who gave their lives for 'King and Country', Worcester was different. The building of a collection of a dozen houses in Barbourne for disabled veterans - appropriately named Gheluvelt Park - formed a more practical memorial to their courageous exploits of long ago.

Above: The Worcester Regiment has long been dear to the heart of the city. Its members were honoured for their gallant exploits during the first world war, while during the second great conflict they fought in North Africa and Burma as well as in Europe. On 15th April 1950, in a ceremony at the County Cricket Ground, 'The Worcesters' were granted the Freedom of the City of Worcester, and presented with a set of silver side drums which bore the Worcester coat of arms, the badge of the Regiment, and the battle honours which dated incredibly from 1694. The Freedom of the City gave the Worcester Regiment the right to march through the streets of the city with drums and bands (and fixed bayonets!) on all ceremonial occasions. As today's youngsters would say - cool! The beautifully crafted drums were heard for the first time that day during the procession which followed the ceremony. That was a red letter day in the

life of the city; a crowd of almost 3,000 attended the memorial service held at the Cathedral, where a memorial to the 579 officers and 10,308 other ranks who lost their lives in the two world wars was unveiled.

Top: No sign of the Technical College, whose building still lay in the future, in this 1940s photograph. Marching smartly along Deansway, a parade of WRAC girls follow their leader, whose three shoulder pips identify her as a Captain, past the Worcester & District Food Office. The image calls to mind not only the necessary ration books but the endless military processions that had become an accepted part of life during the second world war (though as we have no date for this view we cannot be 100 per cent sure that it was still wartime). Back in the 1940s children loved the excitement of the rousing bands and the marching soldiers in their smart uniforms, every one in step. They were a recognised morale-booster, making the average person in the street feel in touch with the forces and the progress of the war; the sound of an approaching band brought people to their doors and children running to march alongside. During the 1940s parades were a regular occurrence, whether the occasion was as grand as a visit from the King and Queen or Winston Churchill, or as ordinary as a meeting of the Boy Scouts or the Girl Guides.

Both pictures: Were you out on the streets on the day that the roars of 'Good old Winnie!' nearly rocked the buildings? Oblivious to the steady drizzle that was falling, the city turned out in full force to give the eminent statesman the welcome he deserved when Winston Churchill visited Worcester to receive the Freedom of the City *(right)*. Every street was decorated with bunting and banners, and Union Jacks flew from every window. With streets wall to wall with people, those who had the opportunity took to their upstairs windows - and some even to the rooftops of buildings! Outside the Guildhall, the crowds whistled and sang to the music played by the Band of the Worcester Regiment as they awaited the arrival of the Mayor and Mayoress - and of course Mr and Mrs Churchill. Predictably, the great man was holding his famous cigar - and responding to the inevitable 'V' sign seen everywhere as the crowds cheered and shouted. The date was 20th May 1950; the war had ended only five years before, and memories were sharp enough to recall the major part this great man had had in ensuring that Britain would come out on top. At the beginning of World War II many had believed that this would be an easy ride and that the conflict would all be over in a few months. But in his speech at the Freedom Ceremony held in the Guildhall the Mayor reminded his hearers that from the day Churchill became Prime Minister in 1940 he had nothing to promise but hardship, blood, sweat and tears - and ultimate victory. It was his brilliant and practical leadership, his grand strategic plans and his stirring speeches that carried Britain through to her 'finest hour'. Churchill's own speech brought a surprise to a few present, who were not aware that one of his ancestors - who also bore the name Sir Winston Churchill - fought in the Civil War on the Royalist side, a subject close to the hearts of the people of Worcester. The deed of admission the Mayor presented to Mr Churchill was contained in a drawer in the ebony plinth of a specially designed jardiniere, which had been created for him at the Worcester Royal Porcelain Works. After the ceremony, Churchill addressed the waiting crowds *(above)*; Lady Churchill can be seen on the left, while the Mayor, Alderman T S Bennett, and the Mayoress are on the right. Both ladies had been presented with bouquets of flowers to mark the occasion. It is his wartime leadership for which Winston Churchill is chiefly remembered today, but he led a colourful and active life not only as a political figure but in active military service and as an author of merit.

Both pages: The Festival of Britain was in full swing when Princess Elizabeth won the hearts of the people of Worcester when she visited the city back in June 1951. The Princess had a sweet smile for Canon A P Shepherd, on her right *(below)*, as they made their way to the Cathedral. What were they chatting about, we wonder? Perhaps he was informing her that the Edgar Tower was built on the orders of King John back in the 13th Century, and that its solid wooden gates were those originally fitted around 800 years ago! Canon G W Briggs, the Sub Dean of the Cathedral, walking on her left, was keeping his thoughts to himself as the memorable scene was recorded for posterity. Princess Elizabeth had wowed the crowds from the moment she arrived in Worcester earlier in the day. The whole city, it seemed, had turned out in full force to give her an uproarious welcome, and her car was at times almost brought to a standstill, so thick were the crowds that day. Looking fresh and pretty in pale blue, the Princess' first visit was to the Royal Worcester Porcelain Works, where

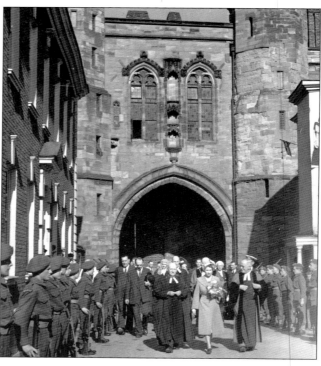

she not only opened the museum with a gold key and made a tour of the factory, but was able to renew acquaintance with painter Harry Davis, who had visited Buckingham Palace in 1948 to get the details of her uniform right for the Royal Worcester figurine of the Princess riding her favourite horse, Winston. Her Royal Highness had a busy and exhausting day. From the factory to the Cathedral *(right)*, where, accompanied by the Mayor of Worcester Alderman William Norton, the Princess made a brief call - to the delight of the hundreds of schoolchildren who were waiting there, eager to catch a glimpse of Her Royal Highness. On the right of the photograph is Lord Lieutenant Admiral Sir William Tennant, who was a Beachmaster at Dunkirk. Then it was on to St Michael's Green, where a detachment of the Worcester branch of the Grenadier Guards Comrades Association was awaiting her inspection. A duty of a more personal kind was awaiting Her Royal Highness as the Worcester Constabulary's Police Sergeant Charles Barford was presented to her. A brave man, he had risked his life to arrest a criminal armed with a

loaded gun - and had earned the King's Commendation for his courageous action. Now he had the praise of the King's daughter also, and Police Sergeant Barford must have been a very proud man that day. The Princess must have been more than ready for tea at the Guildhall, where the Mayor and Corporation were officially presented to her. By the time she left the Guildhall for Shrub Hill station - taking with her the two coffee cups and saucers presented to her by Royal Worcester - the Princess would surely have been exhausted *(facing page bottom)*. She showed no sign of tiredness, however, as she waved goodbye from the royal train.

Princess Elizabeth would soon need all her strength and courage. In September that same year the King's left lung was removed, and in spite of his successful recovery from the operation itself, George VI was still a very sick man; he was in fact suffering from lung cancer (he had been a heavy smoker for many years). At the end of January 1952, Princess Elizabeth and Prince Philip flew to Africa on an official tour, not knowing that they had said goodbye to the King for the last time. He died in his sleep on 5th February - and was genuinely mourned by the whole nation. Elizabeth was crowned Queen on 2nd June 1953.

At leisure

L ike the Pied Piper of Hamelin, the acrobat on stilts attracts the children of Worcester to follow him through the streets of the city. For them the moment is magic: here is a real-life giant to wonder over and giggle at! Full of life and colour and the smell of sawdust, the circus has always been a huge attraction, especially to the youngsters. The antics of the clowns playing pranks on each other - and on members of the audience - has them roaring with laughter, while the high wire act and the graceful trapeze artists keeps them on the edge of their seats. Will the performer lose his balance and slip off the tightrope in front of our eyes? Will the trapeze artist, dressed in her colourful spangled costume, miss the outstretched hands of her partner? All very thrilling stuff, and calculated to send any child home tired and satisfied at the end of a wonderful day out. Bertram Mills Circus was a regular visitor to Worcester - and the kiddies from the local orphanage were always among the audience when the circus came to town.

Right: How nice it is, just once in a while, to do nothing and then rest afterwards, and this charabanc load of day trippers had relaxation and enjoyment on their minds as they set off to who knows where. Everyone loves a day out, especially if the sun shines, and the weather looked reasonably good for this particular party, though they are taking no chances and are wearing their coats and hats just in case. The occasional day trip was a welcome break from the daily routine, whether your day was spent in the office or at the kitchen sink, and once the charabanc was bowling along the sun and wind would blow any workaday blues away. We can only hope that the ladies' hats were safe! The vehicle was convertible, and in the event of rain the fold-down hood would be hastily fixed in place. Was this a church group, we wonder, or a Friendly Society, or even a staff trip? The tradition of staff trips goes back at least a hundred years, and possibly much longer than that.

The scene was recorded for posterity in Angel Place, with the Scala dominating the background. Remember the Scala's beautiful art deco peacocks? Still to be seen today, though the building is now a restaurant.

Bottom: These school children could justifiably claim that their teachers had them 'jumping through hoops' - but it was all in the name of health, strength and physical fitness. At the time, hoops were things you rolled down the street with a stick or you used in PT (physical training) at school, but these same youngsters were destined to live through the hula hoop craze which would hit Britain in the 1950s. Today's elaborate 'PE kit' did not exist back in 1947; the boys' kit was the short trousers and socks they wore all day, while knickers and vests were good enough for the girls! Some other game is in progress behind the hoop jumpers, and close inspection shows us that the young chap standing on the chair has the responsibility of holding up a handkerchief, probably to use as a starting flag or a signal of some kind to the teams. Remember the coloured shoulder bands that identified you as belonging to the blue, red or green team? Those were the days! This was Gorse Hill Primary School two years after the end of World War II; note the old air raid shelter in the corner of the playground; just a few years earlier the children spent many hours here during the daylight bombing raid of 3rd October 1940.

This page and overleaf: You can almost hear the complaints of the children, can't you? 'Daddy - I can't see!' In the 1960s as now, children wanted to see everything that was going on, and Dads the world over have always been ready to provide a shoulder to give their child a grandstand view of an exciting event. There was plenty of excitement on the day of the 1969 Worcester carnival parade, as this fun photograph reveals, and crowds have lined Castle Street to watch the parade of marchers, bands and colourful floats go by *(below)*. Of course the many collection boxes, wielded by ingeniously dressed volunteers, are at the ready, and the people of Worcester dug deep into their pockets, as they did year after year, to provided needed funding for local charities.

There were many imaginative costumes on show that day, and the sign held by the girl displaying pairs of knickers hanging on a clothes line, indicating that she has 'eight draws on one line', would have brought a few smiles from the onlookers as she walked by. 'Around the world in fifty years' proclaims the wording on the display mounted by Metal Castings Doehler that same year *(left)*. They are keen to let the crowd know just how international they really are, and their staff are sporting the costumes of many countries. Here is what used to be known as an Indian chief, but whom the present climate of political correctness advises us would be better called a native American; we have a Chinese 'coolie', a Viking, and a nattily dressed Alpine guide from the mountains of Switzerland. A Roman legionary chats with a little knot of passers by, while the central figure, whose nationality we are unsure of, prepares to go 'up, up, and away' in his beautiful balloon.

A large number of Worcester people were involved in the carnival in one way or another, making costumes, decorating the floats, constructing the props or taking part in the procession. The event has traditionally been a red-letter day in Worcester's calendar, and those people who played no active part in the occasion would turn out to watch, wave and cheer as the parade made its way past them from and to Pitchcroft. Later on there would be time to examine the floats, exchange banter with the gaily

costumed volunteers - and spend your money on balloons for the kids. Is this a young Sea Scout, selling balloons on behalf of BP and the Guide Dogs for the Blind Association at the 1960 carnival *(above)*? At least one mum already has her purse out; her kiddies (is the little boy standing behind also part of her family?) will each go home holding a balloon bearing the charming picture of a dog - unless, of course, some accident on the way reduced them to bits of flabby rubber! All part and parcel of the marvellous fun and frolics of Worcester carnival.

Long ago, photographers would tell young subjects to 'watch the birdie', but the photographer who recorded this scene must surely have substituted 'now all look at your books'! As fascinating as books are, the children so industriously reading in the Junior Library are a little too absorbed for realism.

The date of the photograph is unclear, but it was certainly taken before 1965 as this room was used as a workroom after that time. The display of children's books on the shelves illustrates just how much children's literature has changed over the years. 'Never judge a book by its cover' has been a well-known maxim for many years; in those days you obviously couldn't, as they all look pretty much the same. Isn't it strange, though, that those of us who grew up loving the printed word didn't notice how boring the book covers looked? Today's publishers of children's books have to deal with competition from computer games, the internet, football and television, and books have to be colourful and attractive to look at. And writers are finding that more than ever before they need to spin a yarn that grips a child's imagination from the very first sentence.

Above: 'Nymphs and Shepherds, Come Away'? 'Polly Wolly Doodle'? Or those good old 'British Grenadiers'? Whatever the tune was, this young percussion band is concentrating on getting it exactly right. It would never do to come in at the wrong time and bash your tambourine or tinkle your triangle a bar ahead of all the others! So although the teacher is earnestly conducting the little band, the children would prefer to look down at their music and simply 'make a joyful noise'. These Gorse Hill Primary School children appear to have come to school very smartly dressed for the occasion - they were being photographed for the 1947 Civic Exhibition. The little girls in their pretty dresses, neat hair ribbons and smart white ankle socks; the little boys in shorts and sandals, their hair neatly combed. Little angels, every one - for the time being! We do not need Sherlock Holmes to tell us that this was a warm and sunny summer's day; arms are bare, the windows are wide open, and the great outdoors beckons. Roll on playtime!

Right: Give a child a bowl of water and a few handy pieces of kitchen equipment and he or she will play happily until those metaphorical cows come home. These tots at the local primary school are learning as well as playing, discovering that water poured into a funnel runs out at the other end (perhaps on to the table?), absorbing the fact that a full jug is too heavy for little hands to lift - and finding out that wet sleeves are uncomfortable to wear. If we contrast the scene with the colourful and well-equipped nursery schools of today we might be forgiven for concluding that these children's surroundings could be more stimulating. But after all this was 1947, and Worcester's schools were getting on with the job and using the materials available in post war Britain to the best advantage. The end result, we suspect, would be that these youngsters would develop and flourish, and would be able to read, write and calculate every bit as well as today's kids - and would live to stamp their individual mark upon the world they grew up in. Where are they all now? we wonder.

Shopping spree

Rivals for customers - F R Davis and D W Stevens in Wylds Lane. Many of the goods sold by these two shops were very similar, and presumably if Davis' had not sold foodstuffs and Stevens' had not sold newspapers in addition to sweets and cigarettes they would have found it hard to stay in business! The dispensing machines outside the shops take us back a good number of years: remember Beech Nut chewing gum? And Spangles? Gone but not forgotten! Both shops display a fair number of posters advertising the range of cigarettes they carried. The photograph is dated 2nd November 1964 - just a few months before all cigarette advertising on commercial television was banned. In more recent years all advertisers have found themselves in the position of having to respond to new laws that make it necessary to declare the dangers of smoking cigarettes, and from 1971 the words 'Cigarettes can seriously damage your health' appeared at the foot of all adverts. There were few people about in Wylds Lane at the time of the photograph, though the small girl whose dog has perhaps spotted a cat adds interest to the shot. Where is she now? And what kind of life did she carve out for herself?

hether you wanted underwear, outerwear, or that chic little hat for a special occasion, Gertrude Mitchell's in High Street was once the place to go. The well displayed goods on show in the three windows have attracted a number of passers-by, even though the shop appears to be closed. Their eyes and minds are occupied with window shopping and perhaps choosing a new outfit; did they ever raise their eyes above ground floor level, stand back, and wonder at the fascinating stone carvings between the upper windows high above them? Those carved heads would surely command immediate attention. There must have been a story attached to these effigies; were they the product of the old stonemason's imagination? Or were they representations of living persons? And why were they placed on this building? We will probably never know, but they lend their own touch of mystery to Gertrude Mitchell Ltd's sturdy elegance. To return to our window-shoppers, we notice that one of the ladies in our 1950s shot is wearing a fur coat - still very much a fashion statement at the time, and it would be another decade or so before the tide of public opinion turned against the wearing of genuine fur.

Street (at one time known as With Walk). A nostalgic view, this one, as Paynes was destined to fall victim to the hungry bulldozer, along with the nearby Locomotive Inn, and the adjoining fish and chip shop which had been so handy for a late snack after an evening spent relaxing over a pint or three in the pub! The city's road building programme later gave us a roundabout at this spot.

Top: There was a time when the January Sales could be looked forward to and money put by for the bargains we would undoubtedly find in the shops. They still happen, of course - but so do the 'end of season' sales, the 'closing down' sales and even the 'as good as a closing down' sales, all of which have taken the edge off the good old January kind. Remember queuing outside the door (perhaps with a sleeping bag and a flask of hot coffee), waiting for the shop to open?

This particular January Sale is being held at Witts, the good old-fashioned High Street draper that so many of our readers will remember, and a very few harried shop assistants are doing their best to cope with the massive demand for their service. The lucky few customers - all ladies - have managed to make it to the counter, where they can get a closer look at the bargains on offer. We can almost feel the frustration of those further back, who are obviously dying to examine the goods! Almost every eye is directed towards the items on display, apart from one bored small boy who has spotted the camera. The photograph was taken on 7th January 1966.

Above: A trendily dressed young man props up the wall as he waits for Payne's corner shop to open; was he popping in to stock up on cigarettes for the day? If so, he had plenty of choice in this little general store: Craven A, Players, Park Drive, Benson and Hedges Silk Cut - all were available and well advertised. We can see from the window displays that Payne's was a well-stocked little shop, selling groceries, fruit and vegetables as well as sweets and cigarettes.

The 'corner shop' was an accepted part of life until the advent of large supermarkets drew customers away from their immediate localities and into their out of town facilities. This particular corner shop, snapped back in May 1965, was on the corner of George Street and St Paul's

Shaplands' well-stocked greengrocery shop on the Shambles-Pump Street corner will be well remembered by many of our more mature readers. This shop, piled high with goodies, would have made a good starting place for a lot of local housewives who week after week would pop into town and tour the shops to find the best - and cheapest - apples, pears, oranges, potatoes and Brussels sprouts. The photograph is dated 14th December 1965, and no doubt every one of these shoppers (whose shopping bags are already well filled) had Christmas in mind as they browsed around Worcester's stores. Perhaps a little too early to stock up on sprouts and other perishables, but with only ten days to go before the big day, no doubt many boxes of dates and figs found their way into the shopping bags of these passers-by. Remember BRS? Long gone now, but back in that mid 60s December British Road Services had lots of deliveries to make during the run up to Christmas. This fascinating view of the Shambles, which was more than likely taken from an upper window of P S Fabrics, gives us a real trip down Memory Lane.

Photograph by Michael Dowty

This was the Shambles in August 1968, and although by that time the one-way traffic system was in operation, vehicles were still a problem in what was one of Worcester's main shopping streets. Cars, delivery vans, scooters and bikes - they were all there. But the problem was by no means one-sided - drivers, too, had their difficulties as jay-walking pedestrians unexpectedly stepped into the road without looking! The clock on the wall of P S Fabrics in Pump Street informs us that the time is 12.10pm, and shoppers are out in force, some undoubtedly on their lunch break, to stock up their larders and wardrobes. Towards the left, a father out with his little girl carries one of the 'boat baskets' which were all the rage in the '60s. Others are sticking with the good old shopping bag - and an old-style brown paper carrier with a string handle. When did you last see one of those? On the left is Maggs' well known men's and boys' outfitters.

Below: Did the air raid shelter below the Market Hall once echo to the strains of 'There'll Always be an England' or 'She's my Lady Love' while German bombers droned overhead? This rather bleak scene was captured in 1942, when Worcester was well into World War II. The city escaped the wholesale bombing raids made on Coventry and Birmingham, in fact local families received hundreds of evacuees who came from London and Birmingham to the comparative safety of Worcester. Air raid shelters were a necessary evil all the same, affording much better protection than the deep trenches lined with corrugated iron which had been dug when the late 1930s brought the fear of war to Britain. In spite of Chamberlain's attempts to appease Adolf Hitler preparations had begun to prepare Britain for the conflict.

A shopping arcade has today replaced this mid-19th century Market Hall which many still remember with affection. Ingenious designers, those Victorians; the cast iron pillars supporting the glass roof of the market were hollow so that rainwater could run away into the drains. The fine clock atop the building - illuminated by gas light - was presented to Worcester by Richard Padmore, who was Mayor of the city in 1849.

Christmas shopping. Love it or hate it, most of us do it - and those wise people who plan ahead polish off their present list in good time. After dark, those Christmas lights will twinkle above the Shambles, adding their own touch of seasonal spirit to the scene. The date is 14th December 1963, and the gift-hunting Christmas shoppers are out in full force, dodging the two-way traffic that would only be allowed for another 24 hours. The following day would see the establishing of a one-way system - and about time, too! Today, since the introduction of restricted access, we can cross the Shambles without taking our lives in our hands. Christmas is a boom time for the city's shops and stores, and Woolworths is getting its full complement of gift seekers. Today Woolworths has shed its traditional connection with low prices, but in earlier years the store was a real help to hard-up families, especially during the dark days of depression and unemployment in the 1920s and 1930s. The Woolworths '3d and 6d Stores' were a direct echo of the original '5 and 10 cent' fixed low-price stores that spread in a chain across America at the end of the 19th Century.

A gathering of family and friends appears to be causing an obstruction in Trinity Street as they stop outside Boots to have a chat. The mother of the family has a very large basket with her, resting in the baby's pram as she exchanges news with her friend; we can only hope that the unfortunate child is not somewhere beneath it! This was August 1968, and the same kind of open shopping baskets as our grandmothers carried were still in fashion. How times change! We did not have to worry quite so much back then about our goods being filched as we shopped!

Note how the design of babies' prams has changed over the last 30-odd years. We can note other changes, too, since this nostalgic view was caught by the camera, as this branch of Boots the chemist (together with the adjoining businesses) was demolished and replaced by a large commercial building which is one of those 'love it or hate it' constructions built to resemble a row of small houses. Some are still in the process of making up their minds about the building. At least the 'deception' is an example of innovative design on the part of the architect.

Photograph by Michael Dowty

Making a living

Is it a bird? Is it a plane? No, we can confidently assure the reader that it is neither of these things. What this engine actually *is,* however, remains a mystery, as our extensive investigations and attempts to identify this piece of equipment have drawn a blank. The fascinating and frustrating photograph carries no information and no date, leaving us to formulate our various theories. We know by the funnel, the pressure gauges, a barrow load of fuel, and a couple of shovels that it is steam driven, mend our first conjecture turns in the direction of fire engines. But these young men are wearing the wrong kind of headgear for dealing with fire. Further guesswork leans towards equipment which was used in the Great War. But the theory which has gained the most popularity is that the engine was used to pump away flood water; there was certainly no shortage of water on the day this scene was captured, and the operator is wearing a stout pair of wellies to make sure his feet stay dry. The demonstration drew a sizeable crowd of curious onlookers on the day that FK20 showed Worcester just what it could do. If only it could show us too....

Above: April 1965, and the face of Worcester was about to change as the work on Lychgate Precinct swung into action. Remember those old timber framed houses which used to stand here? Many were glad at the time to see them turned into piles of rubble, as living standards in these tiny homes came far below acceptable levels. But once a piece of history has been destroyed it cannot be brought back, and after the event there was much crying over spilt milk as many who recognised the value of the ancient buildings argued that they could have been renovated and modernised. Sidbury had more that was antique than those old timber framed houses. This was the place often frequented by seekers after antique furniture and jewellery and those looking for the everyday items of yesteryear called in at Philpotts or Taylors to browse among the clocks, whatnot stands, china ornaments, washstands (with marble tops if they were lucky) and all the other paraphernalia of days gone by, while those who had been left that horrid statuette of Great Aunt Maud's could discreetly dispose of it for cash. In fact notices sprinkled liberally around A Taylors' establishment proclaim that top prices were given for genuine antiques.

Above right: A GPO foreman checks the wire tension gauge of a steel wire stretched across the River Severn as engineers prepare for the very first television broadcast from Worcester Races. It was March 1952, and at that time only the more affluent owned a television set. But things were about to change....

Two entire generations have grown up since the small silver screen was introduced into Britain's sitting rooms, but more mature readers will remember the thrill of watching television for the first time. For many - the writer included - this was the Queen's Coronation in June 1953, when those who did not own their own set crowded into the houses of more fortunate neighbours to watch the event. Although Britain had a television service as early as 1936 (suspended during the second world war), few people could afford to buy the expensive sets - and the range of programmes was very limited anyway. Even 13 years on there were only three hours of TV available a day. But by the 1950s sets were beginning to get cheaper, and the Queen's Coronation presented many families with the ideal reason to acquire a TV. In 1960 television licences passed the ten million mark for the first time.

ig a hole in the road and people will gather to stare into it; set up a crane and start moving things around and a crowd will quickly form to watch the proceedings. It's just human nature, after all, and a small crowd of fascinated bystanders are watching as repairs to the railway bridge over Bromyard Road get underway. The placing of this massive girder is the focal point of everyone's attention, from the skilful crane operator to the bowler hatted company managers and civil engineers supervising the work from the side of the track; it is vital that the girder be set down in exactly the right position. The fashions worn here on 14th April 1954 reflect the trend of the day; men's fashions change more slowly than women's, but we note that long macs were still in vogue at the time. The dress of the three ladies on the right is interesting. The 1950s saw the trend move away from the short, material-saving skirts of the 40s, and hemlines moved downwards to mid calf level. It's interesting to note, however, that their hairstyles had not changed much since the end of the war. The style of this toddler's push chair, though, has been replaced in recent years by the modern buggy.

Both pages: 'No hat, no boots, no job' is the well-known slogan that reflects today's emphasis on workers' safety. Seventy or so years ago, however, things were very different, and the flat caps worn by these workers are the hardest hats on site *(below right)*. This was March 1931, and they were widening Worcester Bridge from 24ft to 60ft - a much needed improvement. Back then, of course, employees in many professions undertook many dangerous jobs every day without gauntlets, safety glasses, hard hats or protective clothing of any kind, and reflected very little on the risk factor. These men were, in fact, fortunate to have a job in those tough days of high unemployment, and during that same year, 1931, unemployment benefits were cut by ten per cent and the hated 'Means Test' introduced to examine the personal circumstances of those applying for aid. A national Unemployment Fund had been created in 1928 - the 'dole' of a pitiful sum that was barely enough to keep alive on, yet infuriating to the well-to-do who saw it as encouraging laziness. Unemployment was a subject the Prince of Wales - later to become Edward VIII - had taken to heart, and when he visited Worcester on 28th October to declare the bridge officially open he voiced his concern about unemployment in his speech to a crowd of thousands. Every woman's heart-throb, the debonair Prince used a Royalist sword from the 1651 Battle of

Worcester instead of the more normal pair of scissors to cut through the black and red ribbon across the reconstructed bridge. The city gave him an uproarious welcome, with Union Jacks and garlands of red, white and blue hung across every street. They had no way of knowing that two years on lay the story that rocked the world: in January 1936 the Prince of Wales became King then, 325 days later, renounced the throne for 'the woman he loved'. But Wallis Simpson had been divorced twice, the King was Head of the Church of England - and the Church's teaching on divorce was clear. Edward signed the Instrument of Abdication on the 10th December 1936, and the document was witnessed by his three brothers.

His younger brother Albert - now King George VI - gave him the title Duke of Windsor, and he left England's shores to live abroad, marrying Wallis Simpson the following June. He returned to his native country only a few times during the rest of his life. The newly-widened bridge the Prince opened in 1932 was a great improvement in the life of the city, though there was little traffic about when our second view was captured, looking east *(left)*. Many changes have taken place of course, but readers will recognise a few landmarks such as the Rectifying House on the left of the shot (where the original hoist can still be seen), the recently restored tower of All Saints church on the right, and the terrace of buildings in front of the church. The Infirmary's appeal for contributions for the extension fund still comes over loud and clear, and below it is a notice to motorists crossing the bridge, inviting them to stop and shop in Worcester. Thousands of visitors had been expected in the city, and a special shopping week was planned to run from 28th October - the date of the bridge's opening - to 5th November, with big money prizes on offer. Looking west *(above)*, you will perhaps remember the plans to build a supermarket in Cripplegate Park, and the ensuing campaign to prevent it. In the distance lies New Road, which was raised to a higher level to prevent flooding.

Right: Learning a useful trade is what this picture was all about; these bright young men were taking advantage of the course in bricklaying which was run from Victoria Institute. Their

Below: The end of a long day in the factory, and the first priority of these workers leaving Williamson's Providence Works (one of whom sports the now defunct plus-fours), is to

young arms and shoulders were as yet unseasoned to heavy work, but within a few years - if they went on to make bricklaying their chosen career - they would be heaving hundredweight bags of cement around as if they were feather light! The photograph is one of a collection of post war images put together for a Civic Exhibition held in September 1947. All point to the way Worcester was pushing ahead towards a brighter future. Building was very much a part of those future plans, and these young men would be assured of work for a long time to come. The Corporation's housing clearance scheme had swung into gear before the war, and a steep rise in population during the war years led to an acute shortage of houses. Prefabs presented a temporary solution to the problem, and many people grew to love them; the surprisingly spacious little bungalows with bathrooms, separate toilets, built-in cupboards and drawers and modern kitchens quickly became popular. Prefabs were originally built to last around ten years but in many cities they were still occupied well into the 1960s.

get home. A hot meal will no doubt be waiting - at least for the men - and after that it would be pipe and slippers time, with the old crystal set playing softly in the background. Before long Williamsons would be part of the company founded in 1921 as Allied Tin Box Makers Ltd, which would in turn become Metal Box - a name familiar to us all. During the second world war the factory was engaged on special wartime contracts such as map cases and food cans for the services. We know Metal Box as a major employer in Worcester, and it may be that more than one of our readers will remember working at Providence Works. By the mid 1960s a major extension was being added to another Metal Box factory, but the old Providence Works - one of the company's oldest factories - had seen better days and the decision was made to close it down. Demolition began in January 1970, and today Worcester's new telephone exchange - some say the best modern building in the city - has replaced it.

Photograph by WW Dowty

Jobs for the boys, jobs for the girls: that's how it was in the City Treasurer's Department - as it was everywhere else - in the 1940s. In the Department, it was the girls who worked on the punch card machines (working out the wages?), pictured here in 1947. A male face can be seen in the background, though we have to raise a sceptical eyebrow and wonder if he was there to supervise the ladies and make sure they got it right.... Readers who are too young to remember the almost obsolete punch card machines should know that this was an early form of data processing. Surprisingly, the earliest of these machines was developed as far back as the 1880s by Herman Hollerith for use in the US census. It was not until the country was in the grip of 1960s flower power that girls began to rebel against being relegated to the typewriter, the shop counter or the kitchen sink. Burning their bras (symbolically if not actually), they formed the women's liberation movement and in a male dominated society dared to demand equal rights and opportunities for women. The appointment of Margaret Thatcher as Britain's first female Prime Minister in 1979 was the turning point in many (though not all) occupations.

Both pages: A skilful hand is needed to hand dip Royal Worcester ware. More than five decades have passed since this young lady sitting so uncomfortably at her work was caught on camera *(right)*, but traditional hand dipping still has a place at Royal Worcester today, alongside other more modern methods. After the first firing of the ware, in temperatures of 950°C in the case of porcelain and 1235 ° C in that of bone china, the items are glazed to give them a hard and clean surface. Exactly the right amount of liquid glaze has to be applied to every piece, so the dipper has to make sure that every piece is entirely and evenly covered. Scallop-shell shaped dishes such as the one on the table here are still made at Royal Worcester. Women have long been extensively employed in the pottery industry, from fettling to quality assessment. The better paid workers were the paintresses, whose artistic skills and keen eye for fine detail made them the creme de la creme among the workforce. Yet in those days when equality was as yet undreamed of, even they were not as highly paid as the male employees. Training for the hand painting of fruit can take up to seven years, even today. Slip casting of the more intricate shapes such as teapots, figurines and vases is a traditional technique, and is still used today. Slip - a suspension of clay and water - is poured into moulds, and the excess poured away when the desired thickness of clay has been reached. Once removed from its mould, every item has to be finished and checked for imperfections. These young ladies, pictured in 1947 casting and finishing *(below)*, had good light from a row of windows to work by as well as from the electric lights above. But how their feet must have ached at the end of a long day standing at their benches! The second world war had ended two years before our photograph. During the war a third of the Royal Worcester factory was given over to war work, and by 1945 around 30,000 spark plugs were being produced every week. Today's visitors to the factory can take a fascinating journey through time as they learn about the different processes involved in the production of Royal Worcester ware, view a recreated bottle kiln - and even paint their own plate with the help of one of the company's artists.

This page: Now be honest - can anyone truly remember ever buying gas at a farthing a unit? For the benefit of readers born since decimalisation, there were 960 farthings in a pound. Work it out for yourself! Can today's gas really be more than 700 times dearer than it was when this Worcester New Gaslight Company advertised it as 'the fuel you can afford'? Today's gas, of course, is measured in cubic metres, whereas we can assume that back then it was likely to have been calculated in cubic feet; all we know for sure is that an arm and a leg has been introduced into the pricing structure somewhere along the way....

The same driver, whose name is unfortunately unknown to us, has donned his pristine coat and white cap and poses proudly with each of the Gas Company's two publicity lorries as the event was recorded for posterity. What was the special occasion, we wonder, that called for the designing of these elaborate floats? Possibly the Worcester carnival. Whatever it was, the New Gaslight Company acquitted itself well, and lorry number 51 *(above right)* won first prize for its ingenious display. According to the Company's advertising spiel, install one of these gas fires in your lounge and you could turn the cold days of winter into summer sunshine - a definite attraction in a chilly Worcester January. Readers who remember shivering in the winter mornings of long ago as they waited for their coal fire to take hold and give out some heat, will surely agree. Some may also be unfortunate enough to be able to recall the intricate patterns of lace and ferns which 'Jack Frost' left behind on the inside of their single-glazed windows! But according to the Gaslight Company, theirs was the fuel of the future, giving their customers instant heat and constant hot water, a convenience few were able to experience until post-war prosperity brought a little more freedom and comfort into their lives. Remember the smell which always hung around the gas works down by the Lowesmoor Canal? The backdrop for both photographs is the gas works; the New Gaslight Company were here from the mid 19th Century. The works closed down in 1965 and the bulldozers moved in two years later.

Below: Yes, we have some bananas, to misquote a popular song, and a photographer was on hand to record the sight of armfuls of fruit from warmer climes being unpacked from their railway wagon and loaded on to a truck for distribution. Carefully cushioned with straw packing they would be safe enough on their journey. This was probably the 1920s, when the railway line still ran alongside the river. Not too many years hence lay rationing, and the banana-less years of the second world war. Even when the war ended there was to be no immediate let up in rationing - in fact a year later in 1946 bread went on ration. The same year, however, saw the first bananas that had been available since before the war arrive from the West Indies. Children born during the war had never seen a banana before, and had no idea that they had to peel off the skin before they could eat the fruit. The Home

Secretary went on the radio, giving children instructions how they should open and eat them. The 3rd July 1954 was the day the nation had been waiting for; crowds of people who were sick and tired of coupons gathered in Trafalgar Square and joyfully tore up their much-hated ration books.

Bottom: An intricate network of girders shows us the shape of things to come as construction of the 'new' Post Office - contracted to Wade - gets underway. The year is 1951, and though a number of pedestrians are out and about in Foregate Street the only vehicles in sight are bicycles. One rider, however, can scarcely be said to be riding as he dallies alongside an attractive young lady. We can appreciate his reluctance to set both feet on the pedals and hurry away home! Those were the days long before cycle helmets had been thought of; motor cyclists too took many risks as they rode out completely unprotected. Few of the older men in this view have gone out without a hat, and most of them sport the popular trilby. One nattily dressed gentleman (we simply must label him as such!) is determined to be different, and sports what we can perhaps uncharitably describe as a 'Bill and Ben' hat. Readers who were children during the 1950s will recognise the similarity.... Rain is evidently expected (though the shadows on the ground indicate that the sun is still shining); a few people are either wearing or carrying raincoats, and 'Bill or Ben' has his umbrella.

Delivering the goods

Warehousing and distribution have been around since time immemorial. As soon as mankind switched from a hunter/gatherer economy to living in towns and cities there was a need to establish warehouses. Who built the first warehouse? Who can say - though those readers who went to Sunday school will readily recall that Pharaoh didn't seem at all surprised when Joseph suggested creating stores in which to keep grain from the seven good years as insurance against the seven years of bad harvest which would follow.

It is of course not just storage and warehousing which has a long history - so does distribution. At sea the Romans kept fleets of grain ships to bring corn from Egypt, in those days, despite the occasional famine, the bread basket of the Mediterranean. On land however things were not quite so well developed. In England unless nearby rivers could be navigated, goods were carried by pack horse or less commonly by horse drawn carts. The roads however were usually too poor for carts to be used for long distances. With the 18th century came the age of the canal with pioneers like Thomas Telford providing inland waterways or navigations which made the transport of goods in large volume relatively cheap and effective so helping fuel the industrial revolution. Then came the railways, eventually overtaking the canal system after decades of competition, faster, cheaper and far more exciting. Given the evolution of the transport sector who though would have predicted at the end of the 19th century that before long both canal and railways would be overtaken once more by road transport, that commercial canal transport would be virtually dead and that within three generations many huge railway goods yards would be closed?

Both pages: *The early days of Taylor's.*

Tarmac and the internal combustion engine would sound their death knell and new improved highways would be filled with truck drivers, the knights of the road, taking goods from one end of Britain to the other with a speed and economic efficiency undreamed of by our forebears.

In the years between the wars many fledgling transport businesses were set up as the first generation of trucks and lorries became available on the second hand market for the first time, enabling budding entrepreneurs to buy just one and work for themselves rather for a larger firm. One, now huge, local haulage and warehousing firm Taylors of Martley plc was founded by one such enterprising individual.

A family business since the 1940s Taylors of Martley owes much of its national success to a heritage founded on total commitment.

Demanding nothing short of the very best for its customers the company has maintained the highest levels quality, personal attention and service standards that can only come from family ownership.

That policy has raised Taylors of Martley to the very pinnacle of the modern distribution industry, enabling the group of companies to address every aspect of a first class transportation and administration operation which today includes international haulage, warehousing, transport logistics, contract distribution, vehicle hire and maintenance.

From its headquarters at Edgar House, Martley the company now sits at the hub of a national network of operational centres providing a totally integrated country-wide distribution service with depots in Worcester, Milton Keynes, Yorkshire, Wisbech, Burton on Trent, the Wirral, South Wales and Scotland. But the business has not always been so large.

Edgar Taylor, the father of the present chairman Donald Taylor, founded the company in the dark days of 1940 in the shadow of invasion with the Battle of Britain raging overhead, hardly the most auspicious moment to start a new business; and he started with just one tipper lorry. In those early days this was used to carry logs and coal between

neighbouring villages. Work soon expanded to include transporting gravel from local quarries to aerodromes - a not unsurprising boom industry as more and more airfields were need to accommodate the growing allied fleet of fighters and bombers based on 'the unsinkable aircraft carrier Britain'. Tipper lorries were to be the mainstay of the business both during and immediately after the war: The firm's first flat lorry, a ten tonner, was not purchased until 1954.

Edgar's wife, Gladys, who died in 1997, was actively involved in the business from the outset and was quite willing to drive vehicles as far as the bridge in Worcester in support of her husband's activities - this was as well as bringing up Donald and his three sisters before during and after the war. Back then a female lorry driver was a very rare sight indeed! How many wives today we wonder would put up with such hard work or stand by their man to the same degree whilst he struggled to make a success of his small but growing firm?

Helped by Gladys, Edgar Taylor's firm did grow from these small beginnings with more lorries eventually acquired and through the 1950s the Taylor name

became an increasingly familiar sight on lorries travelling along the area's roads.

E Taylor & Son (Haulage) became a limited company in 1965 with its registered offices at Laughern Villa. In 1988 the name was changed to Taylors of Martley (Haulage) Ltd.

Haulage remains at the forefront of the group's transportation operations; an integral part of which is one of the most advanced information technology systems in the business. Not too long ago delivery notes, invoices, records and work schedules were all written out by hand and once a lorry left the site it and its driver were lost to the world. Today at the centre of the operational network is a fully computerised on-line system monitoring vehicle movements, consignment

Above (both pictures): *Two views of part of Taylor's fleet.*
Left: *The opening of the new offices in 1997.*

Lastly comes Tayhire Ltd which today offers an efficient and user friendly approach to vehicle rental. Flexible rental options have been designed offering a range of choices - anything from a one day hire to a bespoke multi-vehicle long term contract package. Vehicles available include everything from saloon cars to 38 tonne trucks and trailers all available 24 hours a day every day of the week.

tracking, performance and consignment logistics. The haulage company is always in shape to deliver goods both nationally and internationally backed by its state of the art technology. The depot network is operated 24 hours a day, seven days per week with all vehicles supplied with mobile telecommunications for a fast responsive service linked to rigorous quality controls.

D Taylor (Warehousing) Ltd was incorporated in 1976 as a warehousing and storage contractor. Although there have been many changes in the business the warehousing side continues under this name. Storage and handling are an important part of any distribution operation and with years of experience behind it the warehousing company offers the widest range possible of services for every business need. Such services include advanced digital stock control networked through every warehouse providing instant location of individual pallets, itemised movement and automatic stock rotation. Currently the firm operates over a million square feet of modern high bay warehousing with drive through canopies.

Taylors of Martley Plc moved to its present premises at Edgar House, named after its founder, on the Maylite Trading Estate in April 1997. Key customers of the group include Coca Cola, Sainsburys, Friskies, Rover, Rexam and many other major names.

Today senior personnel include Donald Taylor the chairman, haulage director Grahame Taylor, Bruce Maltby Automotive director, Celia Adams financial director, Stephen Taylor managing director and Robert Taylor also a director. As can be seen the Taylor family name remains prominent ensuring that the family traditions of quality and excellence established by Edgar Taylor remain as much to the fore today as they did on that long ago day when he bought his first vehicle.

Yet another element of the group is TM Automotive Logistics backed up by Taylors' distribution network which provides 'total distribution solutions' to the automotive industry.

When next we are driving along the motorway and see a lorry dressed in the livery of Taylors of Martley it will no longer be yet another anonymous truck amongst dozens of others but a reminder of an industry whose rich history goes back for thousands of years. More importantly it will also be a reminder of a firm which has contributed and continues to contribute enormously to the quality of our lives ensuring that the goods we need get where they should be when we want them.

Above centre: *Edgar Taylor.*
Top left: *A riverboat trip for Tayhire employees.*
Top right: *Donald and Margaret Taylor.*

B Smith Packaging - a neatly wrapped package of success

B Smith Packaging of Worcester has grown from a small business run from a house in Droitwich to an international concern, sourcing 80 per cent of its products in the Far East. It remains, however, a family business, in which three generations of Smiths have played their part.It is a rapidly expanding concern, which has gained a reputation for providing quality printed carrier bags, bags and packing material, in both paper and polythene for many prestigious companies throughout the UK.

In the late 1960s Mr RB (Bob) Smith, whilst working for Bowaters, heard a chance comment from an executive at English Electric to the effect that he couldn't obtain polythene to pack certain products. He asked the executive to give him a couple of days, as he might know where such material could be found.

Within two days he went back with a supply of the packing, and B Smith Packaging was started. His father, Basil Smith, founded the firm, as his son continued to work with Bowaters.

Helped by Bob's wife, Carol, and his Mum who sorted out the orders, packed and delivered, after several years it became evident that bigger premises had to be found. An old furniture factory at Crown Street, Worcester, was purchased and the contents of furniture were given to staff and local schools or sold. Young Bob Smith joined his Dad in the company and along with the rest of the family and loyal support from the staff, notably Mr Bert Prosser who

Above: *Mr Basil Smith.*
Below: *The warehouse.*

It was in 1989 that young Bob decided to ask his son, Andrew, who had an engineering degree if he would like to join the company. Crown Works was sold and the company moved to The Farm, and from there more workforce was taken on, notably a young lady who had moved into the area named Di Cope. At this time, Bob and his son, Andrew, decided to source overseas markets and this took place in 1991.

Above: *Overseas container arriving.*
Left: *Some of the firm's products.*
Below: *Seal broken, goods unloaded for storage and distribution.*

gave his all, a fine team came to fruition, and with it expansion of sales.

Crown Works became a hive of activity, and during this period young Bob's son-in-law joined the company for a short time.

B Smith Packaging now supplies a wide range of products. Many major High Street retailers place their customers' purchases at the cash till in Smith carrier bags And no longer are they only made of polythene - paper, hessian and PVC can be provided to suit the customer's wishes, embellished, if desired, with an appropriate name or logo.

When the weary motorway traveller stops for a rest at a service station, buys a snack and a CD to make the journey more enjoyable he or she may well return to the car clutching a package supplied by B Smith. The company also caters

for less glamourous needs in the refuse industry - we are now all aware of the ubiquitous black (or green) plastic sacks in which our household waste is removed.

Companies of all types are well aware of the need to publicise their names as much as possible and B Smith Packaging supply self-adhesive labels,

Above: *Paul Harvey, Sales Director and Assistant.*
Top: *Recent advertising.*
Left: *The sales office.*

Paper comes in a variety of types. As the population in general becomes more aware of environmental issues, the company finds that the demand for recycled paper is growing steadily. Perhaps one associates this with simple, traditional quality,but more sophisticated finishes are of course available, such as embossed, imbossed, ribbed, waxed or film fronted. Similarly polythene is not a simple affair. It can be supplied in low or high density, expanded or co-extruded. And once more the recycled form is in considerable demand.

The Smith family, now including Andrew Smith, has been conscious ever since the founding of the firm in the house in Droitwich that their success is based upon attention to their customers' wishes They are keen to ensure friendly, professional help coupled with an extensive range of products. They are continually reviewing and improving their service and look forward to a bright future.

Left: *Carol, Bob, Nicola and Andrew with Henry the dalmation.*
Below: *Andrew Smith, Managing Director.*
Bottom: *The premises today.*

stickers, name tags and the like to the customer's specification. Charities, too, have turned to the company to supply them with products which will draw the public's attention to their activities.

In order to provide attractive and interesting graphics and pictures on such products, a special design studio has been established. The customer provides an initial brief which specialists work on, followed by consultations and discussions before a final design is agreed upon. Sophisticated computer programmes create eye-catching images, from initial designs through to finished artwork.

Spicers - adding variety to life

The firm now known as Spicers (Builders) Ltd began life when Ernest Vernon Spicer started in business together with his mother under the name of C Spicer & Son in January 1929. Ernest had been a carpenter by trade and had worked in and around the Birmingham area before establishing his own workshop. The first few months of trading obviously gave grounds for optimism and by the December of the same year Ernest had the confidence to branch out on his own and Spicers (Builders) Ltd was formed with Ernest as the founder Chairman.

The firm obtained its start-up capital from the sale of 626 shares of £1 each and building projects in the Worcester area formed the main work-load in the early years and continues to do so.

The first depot was on the junction of Northwick Road and Ombersley Road, Worcester where the office, stores and joinery works were built. The production of high quality architectural joinery has always been a special expertise of the company, building on Ernest's own particular interests and skills.

From small beginnings as a builder the company expanded considerably and in 1942 Mr Fred Chandler joined the

Above: *The letterhead which shows the company's pride in its war-work.* **Right:** *New ambulance station in 1965, now demolished for the new Crown-Gate development.* **Below:** *Worcester College of Education - completed 1965.*

company as Technical Director, an association that lasted until his retirement in 1969. Mr John Chambers, who joined the company in 1964, became Chairman in 1988 until he retired in 1991.

With increased success, the old business premises became ever more inadequate and 1959, the thirtieth anniversary of the founding of the company, was the year when the firm moved to premises more suited to the demands of a larger concern. Everything was transferred from Northwick Road to Checketts Lane, Worcester from where the company still operates to this day.

During the difficult days of the second world war, Ernest Spicer was appointed as County leader for the Ministry of Works defence plan and became responsible for requisition of labour and plant that was required in London to

crematoriums, fire stations, telephone exchanges, hospital extensions and improvements including new operating theatres.

The company has an outstanding record on construction of schools in the City of Worcestre having built, amongst others, Worcester Sixth Form College, Christopher Whitehead Girls' School, Manor Park, Ronkswood, Nunnery Wood Primary, Northwick Manor, Henwick Grove, Rose Hill, St. Clements, Bishop Perowne and Lyppard Grange on Warndon Villages in 1998.

Industrial and commercial construction has included factories for Meco, Carmichaels, Debenhams and Littlewoods Stores and Midland Bank in Broad Street.

In 1989 Spicers provided free contract management for the construction of the workshops at the Cathedral as the first phase of the Cathedral restoration programme.

Social housing has always been important to the company with major projects in Dines Green, Warndon and Blockhouse. These works are now carried out for Housing Associations and Local Authorities.

The company has carried out regular contracts for the National Trust and continues to be on its list of specialist contractors to this day.

Mr Terry Weaver, who joined the company in 1954 and became a Director in 1971 took over as Chairman and Managing Director in 1991. The company continues to thrive locally and employs around sixty people, this in an age where following great changes in the building industry, many national contractors employ far fewer actual employees than Spicers.

Ernest Spicer retired in 1988 and sold the family interest to the senior management, he still lives in Worcestershire where the fruits of his skill and labours are very much in evidence.

rectify damage inflicted on buildings there by Hitler's bombing campaign of the capital. This was clearly a recognition of the quality of Spicer's work and was something of which all involved in the firm could be justly proud. Indeed specially printed company cheques bearing the company name and characteristic trowel logo printed by The Midland Bank Ltd stated at the top 'Contractors to: Ministry of Works, War Office, Air Ministry, Local Authorities'.

Over the years Spicers (builders) Ltd have been responsible for many public and private buildings covering an area from Shrewsbury to Gloucester, Swindon to Hereford. The Worcester Teacher Training College, now Worcester University College was built in 1964 for a cost of £400,000, and Spicers was the main contractor for the Worcester Swimming Pool which was constructed between 1969 and 1971; during the building of this, the company employed more than 250 local workers. They built the Perdiswell Sports Centre in 1981. Apart from these, the quality of Spicers' work can be seen on numerous other public buildings including police stations, churches,

Above: *Greyfriars.*
Top: *Worcester Swimming Pool.*
Right: *John Chambers in 1989 - opening of Cathedral Workshops.*

Keeping order in the Shambles

One of Worcester's oldest surviving family businesses still runs the unique Shambles shop which has been a key visitor attraction of the Faithful City for well over a century.

Pratley's china and glass 'emporium' has always been a veritable curiosity shop - regularly packed with customers curious to savour that remarkable 'times-past' atmosphere within its almost claustrophobic clutter of goods-laden counters. These groan under the weight of vast amounts of china, porcelain and glass, even piled to ceiling level around the walls.

Shoppers venture inside this Aladdin's Cave with trepidation as they walk cautiously along the narrow aisles forming the valleys between the china mountains on each side. Yet, almost miraculously, Pratley's are able to boast that never in their 120-year history have they ever suffered any significant breakages at the careless hands of customers.

Another of Pratley's lucky escapes is never to have suffered a bull in the china shop - amazing really, when one considers that for much of the firm's existence, The Shambles was Worcester's street of butchers! At the peak, there were 20 or more butchers' shops in this historic thoroughfare with slaughterhouses.

For much of the first half of the 20th century, the Pratley family not only had their Worcester base, but also travelled widely around the country as outdoor market traders.

Above (both pictures): *Fanny and George Pratley, who worked in the business together.*
Right: *A picture from when the shop was renamed Winkle and Pratley, Sarah Jane Pratley can be seen centre.*

It is since the second world war that the Shambles shop has also become a Mecca for overseas tourists, especially Americans.

The family firm has prospered over the years from its effective formula of buying quality goods in bulk from Royal Worcester, Royal Doulton and other Midlands potteries in order to gain significant discounts from these wholesale purchases. The benefit has then been passed on to customers in the form of competitive prices which have made Pratley's a big draw with bargain hunters.

The firm was founded at Worcester in the 1870s by Richard Pratley who hailed form the Cotswolds, but came to the Faithful City as a boy. He set up shop at 15 The Shambles but transferred in 1880 to number 16 - the shop which the firm still occupies today.

Richard Pratley and his wife Sarah Jane soon built up a thriving business though, sadly, he died at the comparatively young age of 45. His widow then took up the reins and later married John Winkle, a man from the Potteries.

as teenage boys and girls that the young Pratley foursome joined their parents, later being made partners in the firm, though 'with no say'.

They often went out in the firm's Vulcan lorry to markets all over the Midlands and even further afield, such trips sometimes involving overnight stops at pubs. Annual fairs were also on their regular schedule, including those at Tewkesbury, Ledbury and the Horse Fair at Stow-on-the-Wold.

The late Stan Pratley also fondly remembered the colourful life of yesteryear in The Shambles which was Worcester's 'fresh food centre' with its array of butchers', fishmongers' and fruit and vegetable shops. "We had more laughs in that street than, I imagine, anywhere else in Worcester, and The Shambles also saw a goodly share of affairs, intrigues and even feuds".

Pratley's once counted 'Lords and Ladies and numerous good people' among regular customers and in more recent decades, several stage and screen personalities have called in.

When George Richard Pratley died in 1970 aged 79, his four children took over the firm as partners.

In 1973 Worcester City Council eventually agreed to sell Pratley's the Shambles' shop they had occupied for more than 90 years. More rear land was subsequently bought by the firm in order to create a furniture and carpet sales area.

The four Pratley partners all became familiar local personalities but, sadly, all of them have died over recent years.

The shop was renamed Winkle and Pratley, and Sarah Jane's family grew from two to four children.

Alas, personal tragedy repeated itself for Sarah Jane when her second husband also died young at only 37. She reverted to her former married name and once more ran the business, though now helped by her children.

When she died in 1927 aged 60, Sarah Jane was succeeded as head of the firm by her youngest child, George Richard Pratley who had been born at The Shambles, and therefore 'into the trade'. 'GR' often recalled that he was only 12 when his mother started sending him out to markets with the firm's mobile stall, 'Methods of trading were totally different in those times, and we had to go out to the people to sell our wares. We would travel by horse and dray, regularly visiting every main town and village within a 50 to 60 mile radius. A typical working day would start at 4am with the loading of the dray. It would then be away to market to set up the stall. If you sold out, you went home, but if not, you persevered until the late hours.'

'GR' and wife Fanny were joined in the business by four of their five children - Dick, Stan, Nellie and Nancy. Daughter Jane (now Mrs Sedgley and the only surviving child) chose a different career. It was

The next generation, Richard Pratley, son of Dick, continues the country furniture and tribal rug section of the business, Michael Sedgley, son of Jane Sedgley and Jane Pratley, daughter of Dick also continue the great family tradition, ensuring that an irreplaceable and lasting fixture of the Worcester shopping scene remains for the years ahead.

Top left: *Nellie and Nancy Pratley in the shop.*
Above: *Stan Pratley.* **Right:** *Dick Pratley.*

Clothes of distinction

In today's business world of concrete and chrome Worcester's Armstrongs outfitters is unusual for its setting in Sansome Walk where its club-like interior and quality of service make it well worth a visit.

Armstrongs can trace its trading origins back to the reign of George III. It was however not an Armstrong but one Andrew Graham who was the first member of the family to take on the business which now bears the Armstrong name: he was responsible for moving from Pierpoint Street to the business' present location at Ivy House in Sansome Walk. Ivy House was once the first farmhouse one came to when leaving Worcester. Andrew Graham built the present shop, adjacent to Ivy House, in 1885. The business which he ran from Sansome Walk was that of a 'Scottish Draper' and tea merchant, calling on customers on farms and in their own homes from Shropshire to Gloucestershire.

Andrew Graham was followed by his nephew John Armstrong from whom the business takes its name and who in turn was followed by his niece and her husband Lilian and Robert Hyslop - their son Alec took the helm in 1948. Alec Hyslop was later followed in the business by his son and daughter, Simon and Alexandra.

Over the years one of the biggest changes in the clothing industry was the introduction of ready-to-wear clothes at the expense of the bespoke or made-to-measure trade. Ready made clothing had been introduced in the 1920s, then almost all made in this country.

During the second world war clothes rationing was introduced. In one period 18 coupons were given to adults, whereas 26 coupons were needed for a man's three piece suit. This meant other members of the family having to give up some of their coupons.

After the war European fashions were introduced to Worcester by Armstrongs. Today, European clothes dominate the clothing on offer: Atelier Torino by Konen of Munich, Baulmer of Austria, Point, Paul and Shark of Italy and Eton of Sweden are favourites at Armstrongs. In the ladies' showroom again the continentals shine with names such as Basler, Sommerman, Gerry Weber and Rodier to the fore.

Above: *(Oval picture) Andrew Graham, (Square picture) John Armstrong.*
Below: *Three Counties Show - 1933.*

In the last fifty years other important changes have taken place: lighter clothes, mixtures of fibres have led to minimum ironing and easy washing. Also of great significance reflecting our increasingly affluent lives has been an upgrading of sizes in men's and women's clothing; for example in 1946 men's suits were stocked sizes up to a 46 inch chest - now it is 54 inches and rising!

Armstrongs' travellers were calling on customers until the 1970s when it was found unnecessary since many farmers' wives had their own cars and became independent of travelling salesmen. Grocers, coal merchants and as well as tailors all largely curtailed their travelling during this period as more and more customers were able to come to them.

A sense of tradition though is important and this can be readily seen and appreciated by visitors to Armstrongs: it is however very necessary to keep abreast of the times. Though bespoke tailoring remains important at Armstrongs this has now been augmented by the computer. Customers can choose from the same wide selection of clothes as in traditional tailoring but measurements and adjustments are sent by computer to Strasburg where suits are cut by laser and tailored using customers' choices of lining and buttons before being delivered to Worcester within 15 working days.

One area of growth has been the hire of formal wear. Black and grey morning suits at the beginning of the hire business were followed later by the introduction of frock coats, Prince Edward jackets, cream embroidered coats and a galaxy of fancy waistcoats. Here, as in other departments, success has depended on service and attention to detail, making the customer feel special.

Besides Worcester there is also Armstrongs in Broadway, a small shop in the High Street, with its special character serving the Cotswolds - being situated in such a beautiful village it attracts visitors from all over the world many of whom keep in touch on their return home.

Armstrongs has come a long way since Andrew Graham first travelled the highways and byways to sell his wares.

Above left: *Armstrong's premises today.*
Top: *Armstrong's horse and cart which was a familiar sight between 1954 and 1970.*

93

Educational excellence since 1883

The Alice Ottley School has been a centre of excellence for the education of girls in Worcester since its foundation in 1883. Originally named the Worcester High School for Girls, it was renamed in 1914 in honour of its first headmistress, Miss Alice Ottley. The aims and aspirations of its founders, "to awaken interest in study for its own sake, to develop training of character, and to help girls be aware of others" still underpin school life today. Education for girls was the subject of much discussion in the 19th century and following the radical views of Miss Buss and Miss Beale parents began to think more carefully about their daughters' education.

Under Miss Ottley's guidance the school quickly attained high academic standards; examination successes were impressive and before long many old girls had gone on to obtain university degrees, including from Oxford and Cambridge.

In 1887 Mr Edward Elgar was placed on the list of visiting masters for the violin. He gave new vitality to concerts, bringing his immense talent for orchestration to the arrangements of all sorts of works. He was then working on 'The Dream of Gerontius' and occasionally brought the score to the school and played passages to a few of the young teachers.

As the city of Worcester was growing in the 1880s, so too did the school, and in the period up to the first world war a building programme was established to provide accommodation for the increasing number of girls. The school's reputation for academic excellence and all-round education grew with it.

Over the last hundred years the school has continued to adapt and develop to meet the ever changing educational needs of its pupils and the demands of society. The school roll has grown to over 600 and it is one of the leading independent day schools for girls in the Midlands.It provides continuity of education from the age of 3 to 18 and in partnership with parents, the aim

Above: *Miss Alice Ottley, headmistress 1883 - 1912.*
Below: *The Alice Ottley School, 1923.*
Bottom: *Miss Ottley and the first students, 1883.*

aspects of theatre. A thriving Art department is the centre for individuality and flair across a wide range of media.

Education, of course, extends beyond the curriculum and the pupils have fun and enjoy a wide range of extra-curricular activities from dancing to debating, photography to public speaking.

is to enable each girl to develop her individual talents and to reach her full potential. Springfield (the Junior School), the Senior School and the Sixth Form Centre housed in St Oswald's Lodge, all offer excellent accommodation. A modern science block and a well equipped technology suite provide good facilities for Chemistry, Biology, Physics and Technology teaching. A newly furbished wing accommodates a thriving Modern Languages Department and excellent facilities for the teaching of Home Economics and Textiles.

The good relationship which exists between staff, students and their parents is a strength of the school. In a sympathetic atmosphere of care and support, girls are able to have fun and work hard. There is regular co-operation with the nearby boys' school - the Royal Grammar School Worcester - through joint participation in music and drama productions, activities, lectures and outings.

On the lacrosse pitch, in the modern sports hall, on the hard courts for tennis and netball and in the adjacent City of Worcester sports centre, The Alice Ottley girls enjoy a tremendous range of sporting activities. A tradition of excellence in the Creative and Performing Arts is well established. Music enjoys a reputation of which the school can be proud as the girls are encouraged to join school orchestras, choirs and instrumental groups There are also workshop and major school productions which give the girls opportunities to develop their talents in all

At the end of their education at The Alice Ottley School, the students are ready to face the challenges of the wider world with a high degree of confidence and independence. The majority of them go on to Higher Education, embarking on a wide range of courses from Anthropology to Physiotherapy and from Classics to Medicine. The strong links with the Old Girls' Association are evident in the many letters and visits received from former pupils of all ages and the number of former pupils who choose The Alice Ottley for their daughter.

Top left: Vanessa Redgrave (left) at a school fete in 1961. Top right: Sheila Scott (ex pupil) before beginning her world flight in 1966. Right (both pictures): The Alice Ottley School today.

Robin Elt Shoes - A tradition of fine footwear for five generations

If you live anywhere near Worcester the words Elt and shoes will be synonymous to you. It is also highly likely that your parents bought shoes from Robin Elt's father and their parents bought shoes from his grandfather or even great-grandfather. A well-known Victorian saying was "never stint on your bed or your shoes because if you are not in one you will probably be in the other!"

Having taken a degree in Biology at Exeter University, Jenny Elt decided that the pull of the family business was too strong to resist. When she joined the business in 1991 she represented the fifth gener-ation as one of Worcester's most famous family names with a heritage in footwear stretching back to 1872 and beyond.

Albert Edward Elt created the Elt tradition by taking over the shoe shop in Worcester in 1872 from one William Weobley. Albert sold shoes, boots and originated the famous Black Bess brand of boot polish from what was then Hills Boot Stores in Worcester's High Street. Bert and Ada Elt, proud suppliers of footwear to Edward Elgar, traded in that same High Street shop, roughly where River Island stands today. They were joined in the 1930s by their son Roy - Jenny's grandfather. Perseverance was the hallmark of the Victorian age and Ada stayed as a cashier in the Worcester shop until the age of 91!

After the second world war Roy assumed full control of the family business - with a clear recognition from the outset that the hallmarks of quality products linked with timeless classic styling was the way forward. He had the vision to transform a small mediocre property into a flagship shoe store whilst being surrounded in those days by butchers, pubs, greengrocers and fishmongers!

His vision also extended into recognising the opportunities in various other towns and he started his expansion programme in 1948 by moving into Malvern, which is now the current head office of Robin Elt Shoes. More branches were added, both in Worcester and nearby towns as opportunities arose. Roy's son Robin joined the team of his father and grandmother in 1964 and was immedi-ately despatched to Crockett & Jones in

Above centre: *Albert Edward Elt in a picture dating from 1895, with son Bert.*

Northampton to learn 'proper shoe making'. At that time he became a Bespoke Shoemaker and still proudly shows the first pair of shoes he made.

In 1969 Roy merged his business interest with the Church Group's retail division. Robin continued to run the Worcester shop in the 'hands on' Elt tradition, at the same time being responsible for a dozen or so Church shops in the locality. On becoming branded Buying Director for the whole group, Robin quickly realised the increasing inflexibility of multiple trading.

With the Church Group's support, Robin took back the family shops in Malvern and Leominster to resume independent retailing in 1991. A branch in Torquay was opened in 1992, Lychgate (Worcester) in 1997, an Ecco concept store in the Shambles in 1998 and most recently a new store in Evesham. The Elt aim is to offer a wide range of the very best classic footwear sourced from around the world but led by the finest English makers such as Barker, Church and Van Dal. Shoes that reflect today's casual lifestyle where comfort benefits abound and the investment is protected by both the brand name and timeless classic styling. As Coco Chanel once said, "when fashion fades - only style remains". Their staff, who are a key asset in the firm's continuing success, offer a professional, informed yet friendly approach.

The Elt name quite simply equates with quality and style and has built up a loyal customer base.

Long gone are the days when Edward Elgar requested ankle length glace kid button boots and Mrs Elgar requested Louis heel courts with the finest chamois leather lining. Today's customers are fashion conscious but not fashion victims. They appreciate the adventures of daily life and are fully prepared to face them with the appropriate footwear for every eventuality and occasion.

The reputation just keeps on growing. On the opening of the new Evesham store, many country folk have recounted fond tales of both great-grandmother Ada and grandfather Roy Elt and their various journeyings and talks throughout the Worcestershire countryside.

So why is the Elt business so different? Robin and Jenny have a passion for shoes. They want you, their customer, to share the joy of experiencing, quality, style and comfort from around the world. Above all they want you to have fun with your shoes. As the years go by, however, whatever the vagaries of fashion and our own changing inclination, the one tradition that will keep up with us, as it has during the two previous centuries, is Worcester's most famous footwear name - Robin Elt Shoes - perhaps the family name with the longest trading history in Worcestershire?

Above centre: Early advertising for Black Bess boot polish. Below left: Robin Elt. Below right: Jenny Elt.

Froude Consine - a measure of power

One of the great triumphs of Britain and the British was the development in these islands of the science of engineering throughout the 18th, 19th and 20th century. The practical application of science by men who were interested in how things worked led to the machines and inventions which fuelled and sustained the industrial revolution and in the process helped make Britain the workshop of the world.

One of Worcester's most prominent engineering companies, Froude Consine, can trace its origins back to one of the late Victorian era's most practical of mechanical engineers: William Froude.

It was in 1877 that William Froude invented the hydraulic dynamometer. It was not though until four years later, in 1881, that the partnership of Hammersley Heenan and Richard Froude, William's son, were able to produce the first commercial version of Froude's invention. The hydraulic dynamometer had been developed by William Froude in response to a plea from

the Admiralty desperately in need of a means of absorbing and measuring the power outputs of huge new naval engines. The neat engineering solution arrived at by William Froude is still in use today emphasising the brilliance of his mind.

The firm of Heenan and Froude were however primarily structural engineers the demand for dynamometers being naturally somewhat limited, and other projects dominated the firm's books. The grandstand at Epsom race course and Blackpool Tower being but two of the major contracts obtained in those early days, both still standing as monuments to the company's skills.

Above left: *William Froude.*
Above right: *The first hydraulic dynamometer.*
Below: *An early Heenan & Froude car tester.*

Heenan & Froude moved to Worcester in 1903 and soon extended the range of equipment being produced to include equipment to test engines in ships, cars and eventually aeroplanes.

Soon the firm was producing complete test rigs to simulate road conditions followed by similar rigs to test tyres, brakes, gear boxes, back axles and in later years plant for testing propeller engines and, much later, turboprop and turbojet aero engines.

The firm continued to diversify down the years. By the time it became Redman Heenan International Ltd in 1968 the product range in addition to test plant included industrial and municipal incinerators, coolers, variable speed drives and metal forming machines. To cope with that wide range of activities action was taken to rationalise the products into manageable specialities.

To streamline management and production further it was decided towards the end of 1973 to divide the products into four separate self-accounting divisions and, early in 1974, the largest of these, the test plant division was moved with all production facilities to a modern factory at Gregory's Bank. Subsequently the four divisions were formed into individual subsidiary companies of Redman Heenan International giving each a stronger identity. As a result the Test Plant Division became Froude Engineering Ltd giving prominance to the name of the man on whose innovative brilliance the company was founded. In 1976 the firm gained the Queen's Award for Technological Achievement for its 'F' range of computer controlled dynamometers.

By 1981 the business, still under the name of Froude Engineering Ltd and operating from its factory in Gregory's Bank celebrated its centenary. The Consine part of the present company's name arrived in 1983

when Consine Dynamics joined Froude Engineering Ltd to form Froude Consine as a market leader in engine and vehicle test technology.

In 1995 the firm relocated to modern facilities at Blackpole Road where it is well equipped to service the test requirements of automotive, marine and aerospace customers around the world.

In 1996 Froude Consine acquired Hofman Prueftechnik and Brush ATS to establish Froude Automotive Test Products. FATP provides one stop sourcing of the design and supply of engine and vehicle test equipment for Research and Development, production and quality validation to the world's automotive industry.

Today Froude Consine has a range of hydraulic, eddy current and alternating current dynamometers as well as vehicle emission and mileage accumulation chassis dynamometers, all with matching PC-based digital controllers and data acquisition systems.

No doubt William Froude, were he to return to the company that bears his name, would have difficulty recognising some of the products, not least the high tech electronic wizardry which is now so evident. What Froude would however recognise instantly is a continuing commitment to innovation - his greatest legacy of all!

Top left: *A modern engine test cell.*
Top right: *Chassis dynamometer and automatic robot driver.* **Right:** *Brian Hemstock, MD and the Worcester premises today.*

From bicycles to Builders Merchant

Where did Capability Brown get hold of the building materials and landscaping supplies he needed we wonder? Things cannot have been easy in the past: in those far off days builders could not pop down to the local builders merchant and find everything they could possibly need under one roof. Today, however, Brown could simply go along to Worcester's Bullock Buildbase and stock up.

Buildbase is one of the UK's fastest growing builders merchants. All of its many branches are long established companies in their own right each one of which has been serving local trades people for many years, with experience and knowledge to match.

Worcester's branch of Buildbase, Bullock Buildbase, is today located on the Diglis Trading Estate.

The Bullock Buildbase company was originally called F Bullock (Hauliers) Ltd founded by Frederick Bullock. As far back as the early 1900s Frederick Bullock had managed a bicycle shop in Worcester. The Bullock family haulage business began in 1938 with premises in Coombs Road, Worcester. The company started its life as haulage contractors with a fleet of small 5 ton tipper lorries carrying construction materials, ashes

*Above: A driver with one of the early vehicles. **Right:** A vehicle transporting metalwork. **Below:** Frederick Bullock, pictured right, with one of his drivers and lorries.*

from local power stations and, during the hot summer months, gritting the roads.

The company was established just before the outbreak of the second world war which created many difficulties not least the rationing of fuel. In addition there was a shortage of building materials which meant that much of the firm's first premises had to be constructed using second hand materials, some of which were reclaimed from an old nunnery. The gothic arched windows were a notable feature of the office block!

was by then a major and respected supplier of materials to builders and landscapers in Worcester and the surrounding areas, with an enormous range of paving and walling materials, aggregates and natural stone. This concentration of the company's activities led to the new trading title of Bullock Building and Landscaping Supplies during the 1990s before the business was finally acquired by the Oxford-based Buildbase Group becoming Bullock Buildbase.

Business grew and Gerald Bullock joined his father in the 1950s and went on to become Managing Director in the late 1960s. Company vehicles were involved in many of the major construction projects carried out in Worcester during this period including the Lichgate and Blackfriars Shopping Centres and the building of the M5 motorway. Gerald also diversified the company's activities setting up Worcester's first skip business and beginning to stock and sell building materials. He had a great interest in landscaping materials and the company became well known for the range of the products stocked and the expertise of its staff. The company also became involved in plant hire, waste paper recycling and scrap metal.

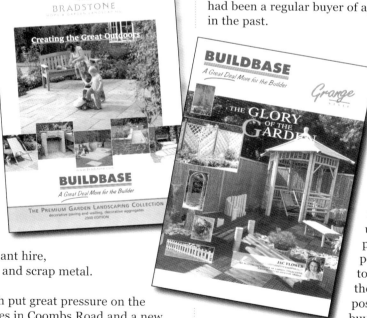

The company's growth put great pressure on the small 1/3 acre premises in Coombs Road and a new site was acquired in 1974 at Navigation Road on the Diglis Trading Estate. It was here that the company began to focus on its role as a builders' merchant; the Coombs Road site was eventually sold in 1986 for redevelopment.

Clive and Nigel Bullock, the third generation of the family to work in the business joined their father Gerald in the 1970s and 80s respectively. The company

As a new Buildbase branch there was extensive refurbishment work carried out in the main building to create a bright new sales counter and sales area approached via a landscaping products display. A kitchen and bathroom centre has been built and new racking installed in the yard. A timber shed and mill facility will complete the transformation in late 2000.

Ten staff work with the new manager Tom Morse who had been a regular buyer of aggregates from Bullock's in the past.

Nigel Bullock the founder's grandson left to take up a key role as landscape development manager based at the Redditch branch of Buildbase.

Buildbase is part of the Grafton Group plc committed to the manufacture and distribution of building products. Its huge buying potential ensures its ability to always offer customers the most competitive price possible whether they are buying timber, bricks, roofing products, plumbing supplies, kitchens, bathrooms or garden products ranging from paving slabs to wheelbarrows and fences.

Capability Brown would have loved it!

Top: *Part of Bullock's plant in the 1970s.* ***Above:*** *Two recent brochures showing just a small selection of the stock that Buildbase carry.*

A Jewel in the crown

Diamonds are a girls best friend. But then so are rubies and emeralds, gold and silver; not to mention pearls. Indeed it was the lure of freshwater pearls, amongst our many other assets, which first attracted the Roman legions to the shores of Britain.

Today a pearl amongst Worcester's retail outlets is the jewellers A Forrest-Hay, founded in 1976 by Anthony Forrest-Hay. After leaving public school in 1965 he had at first worked for his family's own manufacturing company in Hockley, Birmingham's jewellery quarter, a family business which had been established in 1860.

At the same time Anthony attended Jewellery College learning the skills of the trade. After leaving college Anthony worked 'at the bench' for six years before joining a London retail jewellery company to obtain experience. Having enjoyed the experience of retailing and having successfully completed the National Association of Goldsmiths two year course of examinations, he decided to open his own jewellers in Worcester, finding premises at 31 The Cross, High Street. Within a few years he had also opened a second store and a coffee shop in Droitwich.

In the following years, despite the rigours of four economic recessions, Anthony, helped by his wife and three daughters, developed the business selling modern and traditional jewellery, buying gold and jewellery and providing an independent valuation service. The firm specialises in good quality second-hand jewellery, watches and repair services. New items of jewellery are created by goldsmiths and silversmiths selected for their quality of work and value for money.

Another speciality developed over more than ten years is selling unwanted second hand jewellery on behalf of customers.

Clients bringing their unwanted jewellery for potential sale are professionally advised on the expected price which might be obtained. Selling on behalf of customers in this way allows clients to achieve a much higher price than would be normally offered at auction or over the counter, and for the buyer the price reflects a smaller profit margin. Items are sold on a commission basis with no charge if no sale is made.

A Forrest-Hay Ltd has certainly made itself into a jewel in Worcester's crown!

Below: *The current shop frontage.*
Bottom: *The shop at 31 The Cross, High Street, Worcester as it was in the mid 1970s.*

Nearly a century and a half of top quality and reliability

Ebenezer Baylis gets it right first time, every time. That will come as no surprise to the mail order market and educational publishers who form the core of this company's business. The firm has been in the printing and binding trade for nearly 150 years. Leaflets, booklets, catalogues and directories are printed in a variety of colours and bound together using several techniques. State of the art machinery ensures an efficient and swift process. Some four generations of the family have been involved in expanding and developing a company that also produces re-usable stickers, folders and write-on and wipe-off books.

What Ebenezer Baylis would have made of the 21st century and its dotcom demands is difficult to imagine. Queen Victoria was still in the first half of her reign when, in 1858, with one treadle platen and debts of 15/6d (77.5p), he founded his one man printing business at 77 The Tything. On leaving his first premises he organised a raffle to clear his old stock when he moved to 22 The Cross; such raffles were immensely popular and the police had to be called to deal with the crowds!

By 1935 the Baylis enterprise had moved to purpose built premises on the outskirts of Worcester. During the second world war half the factory was turned over to the production of covers for aircraft fuel tanks. In 1943 a fire at the factory did £50,000 worth of damage but as a result of the firm's involvement with war work the premises were rebuilt within a few months.

Lithographic work was included after the war when the specialist company of Fleming and Humphreys was acquired.

By the 1960s 75 per cent of the company's output was devoted to book printing. One of its most notable publications was Winston Churchill's six volume 'The Second World War' that required over 1,000 tons of paper, 10 tons of ink and 20 tons of metal to get it onto the bookshelves. In 1963 Ebenezer Baylis became part of the Great Universal Stores empire and the company continued to grow into the major concern it is today.

Left: A company letterhead from the early 1900s.
Top: The Composing Department in the 1930s.
Below: Some of the hundreds of titles currently being produced by the firm.

These young ladies, pictured in 1947 casting and finishing had good light from a row of windows to work on their Royal Worcester ware

Acknowledgments

The publishers are grateful to the following organisations and individuals for allowing us to reproduce photographs from their collections:

John Stafford of Worcester Library, Worcestershire County Council for access to photographs at Worcester City Library, Elizabeth Dowty for kindly allowing us to reproduce photographs taken by her late husband, Michael Dowty, Geoffrey Hopcraft of Worcester.

Thanks are also due to
Peggy Burns who penned the editorial text and
Steve Ainsworth for his copywriting skills